This side of our handy tear card shows you the Flash toolbox containing all of the drawing, painting and selection tools available in Flash, as well as the view options, color options and specific tool options. The letter seen in parentheses next to the name of the tool is the keyboard shortcut for that tool. The Options portion of the toolbox for each tool selected is shown below to help you quickly select the correct tool for your task, based on the available options.

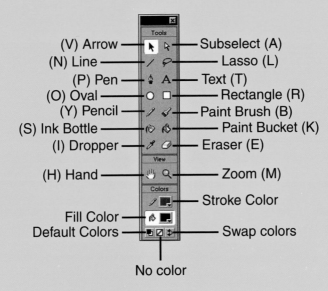

(V) Arrow — Subselect (A)
(N) Line — Lasso (L)
(P) Pen — Text (T)
(O) Oval — Rectangle (R)
(Y) Pencil — Paint Brush (B)
(S) Ink Bottle — Paint Bucket (K)
(I) Dropper — Eraser (E)

(H) Hand — Zoom (M)

Stroke Color
Fill Color
Default Colors — Swap colors

No color

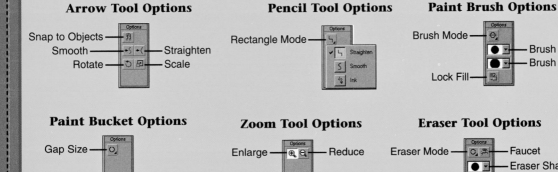

Arrow Tool Options

Snap to Objects
Smooth — Straighten
Rotate — Scale

Pencil Tool Options

Rectangle Mode
Straighten
Smooth
Ink

Paint Brush Options

Brush Mode
Brush Size
Brush Shape
Lock Fill

Paint Bucket Options

Gap Size
Lock Fill — Transform Fill

Zoom Tool Options

Enlarge — Reduce

Eraser Tool Options

Eraser Mode — Faucet
Eraser Shape

Rectangle tool options

Round Rectangle Radius

Special Flash Keyboard Shortcuts

The following keyboard shortcuts are not used generally in Windows or with Macs, but will make life easier as you edit Flash movies.

Windows Shortcut	Mac Shortcut	Action
Ctrl+Shift+S	Cmd-Shift-S	Save As
Shift+F12	Shift-F12	Publish
Ctrl+Shift+V	Cmd-Shift-V	Paste in Place
Ctrl+Alt+X	Cmd-Option-X	Cut Frame
Ctrl+Alt+C	Cmd-Option-C	Copy Frame
Ctrl+Alt+V	Cmd-Option-V	Paste Frame
Ctrl+Alt+Shift+O	Cmd-Option-Shift-O	Outline
Ctrl+Alt+Shift+F	Cmd-Option-Shift-F	Fast View
Ctrl+Alt+T	Cmd-Option-T	Timeline
Ctrl+Shift+W	Cmd-Shift-W	Work Area
Ctrl+Alt+Shift+R	Cmd-Option-Shift-R	Rulers
Ctrl+'	Cmd-'	Grid
Ctrl+Shift+'	Cmd-Shift-'	Snap to Grid
Ctrl+Alt+G	Cmd-Option-G	Edit Grid
F8	F8	Convert to Symbol
Ctrl+F8	Cmd-F8	Insert Symbol
F6	F6	Keyframe
F7	F7	Blank Keyframe
Ctrl+I	Cmd-I	Instance
Ctrl+F	Cmd-F	Frame
Ctrl+Shift+Up Arrow	Cmd-Shift-Up Arrow	Bring to Front
Ctrl+Up Arrow	Cmd-Up Arrow	Bring Forward
Ctrl+Down Arrow	Cmd-Down Arrow	Send Backwards
Ctrl+Shift+Down Arrow	Cmd-Option-Shift-Down Arrow	Send to Back
Ctrl+G	Cmd-G	Group
Ctrl+Shift+G	Cmd-Shift-G	Ungroup
Ctrl+B	Cmd-B	Break Apart
Ctrl+Shift+P	Cmd-Shift-P	Plain
Ctrl+Shift+B	Cmd-Shift-B	Bold
Ctrl+Shift+I	Cmd-Shift-I	Italic
Ctrl+Shift+L	Cmd-Shift-L	Align Left
Ctrl+Shift+R	Cmd-Shift-R	Align Right
Ctrl+Shift+C	Cmd-Shift-C	Align Center
Ctrl+Shift+J	Cmd-Shift-J	Justify
Ctrl+L	Cmd-L	Library

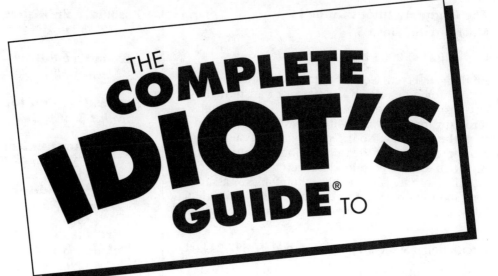

THE COMPLETE IDIOT'S GUIDE® TO

Macromedia®
Flash 5™

David Karlins

with artwork by Paul Mikulecky

A Division of Macmillan Computer Publishing
201 West 103rd Street, Indianapolis, Indiana 46290

**The Complete Idiot's Guide to
Macromedia Flash 5**

International Standard Book Number: 0-7897-2442-1

Library of Congress Catalog Card Number: 00-103412

Printed in the United States of America

First Printing: *November 2000*

03   02   01   00   4   3   2   1

Trademarks

Warning and Disclaimer

Associate Publisher
Robb Linsky

Executive Editor
Beth Mullett

Acquisitions Editor
Heather Banner Kane

Development Editor
Laura Norman

Managing Editor
Thomas F. Hayes

Project Editor
Leah Kirkpatrick

Copy Editor
Kate Givens

Indexer
Sheila Schroeder

Proofreader
Harvey Stanbrough

Technical Editor
Paul Mikulecky

Illustrator
Judd Winick

Team Coordinator
Julie Otto

Interior Designer
Nathan Clement

Cover Designer
Michael Freeland

Production
Steve Geiselman
Brad Lenser
Liz Johnston

Contents at a Glance

Contents

xi

About the Author

David Karlins writes, teaches, and consults on Web graphics and Web design.

David's recent books include the *FrontPage 2000 Bible* (with David Elderbrock), *MCSD: Designing & Implementing Web Sites Using Microsoft FrontPage 98*, *Teach Yourself FrontPage 98 in a Week*, *Wild Web Graphics with Microsoft Image Composer*, and *Teach Yourself CorelDRAW 9 in 24 Hours*.

David's Web site at www.ppinet.com provides advice, resources, and forums for Web and graphics designers.

Contributing artist **Paul Mikulecky** is the owner of the award-winning Electronic Design Studio. He is a graphic designer, illustrator, and designer of Flash movies for many commercial Web sites.

Dedication

This book is dedicated to to my dad, Sheldon Karlins—a creative spirit all his life.

Acknowledgments

This book incorporates much that I've learned from teaching Web design classes and working with clients creating Flash movies. Thanks, everyone. You'll all see a little of yourselves in the tricks, tips, and advice I've included in this book.

Paul Mikulecky's artwork provided an important contribution to this project. His illustrations somehow managed to combine the coolest stuff Flash can do with easy, accessible techniques that work great in this Complete Idiot's Guide.

All the editors who put this book together did a wonderful job. Special thanks go to Laura Norman and Heather Kane. They were truly committed to putting out a useful, entertaining, and fun book, and worked long and hard to make it happen.

Thanks also to my agent Lisa Swayne for helping make this book possible, and to Beth Millett at Que who helped launch this project.

Tell Us What You Think!

As the reader of this book, *you* are our most important critic and commentator. We value your opinion and want to know what we're doing right, what we could do better, what areas you'd like to see us publish in, and any other words of wisdom you're willing to pass our way.

As an Executive Editor for Que, I welcome your comments. You can fax, email, or write me directly to let me know what you did or didn't like about this book—as well as what we can do to make our books stronger.

Please note that I cannot help you with technical problems related to the topic of this book, and that due to the high volume of mail I receive, I might not be able to reply to every message.

When you write, please be sure to include this book's title and author as well as your name and phone or fax number. I will carefully review your comments and share them with the author and editors who worked on the book.

Fax: 317-581-4666

Email: desktop_pub@macmillanusa.com

Mail: Beth Millett
          Que
          201 West 103rd Street
          Indianapolis, IN 46290 USAFore

Foreword

Turn back the clock seven years, and you'll see a World Wide Web that was pretty simple. HTML was easy and we could all do it, sometimes to the consternation of our pets and friends who suddenly found pictures of themselves on our Web sites for all the world to see! And that's what was wonderful about the Web[md]we could express ourselves easily and have fun exploring our creative instincts.

Since then, in compliance with the laws that seem to govern the growth of all technology, things have become much more complicated. From JavaScript to databases, Web technologies have advanced rapidly as we seek to create more exciting, more interactive content. Probably the most popular technology right now for creating dynamic Web content is Flash. This wondrous Macromedia product began as a fairly simple tool for creating animations based on vector graphics, but with each new version, its learning curve has increased to a steep incline that can strain the heart!

But fear not. With humor, and with an eye toward simple explanations, David Karlins has crafted an excellent guide to the intricacies of Flash 5.0. Nothing beats having someone hold your hand and walk you step-by-step through the process of creating all kinds of different animations with interactive and multimedia components. So dive in and explore the world of Flash. You'll be amazed at what David will have you doing, and you won't regret a moment of the time you spend with this book.

Christopher Marler
Director
San Francisco State University
Multimedia Studies Program
msp.sfsu.edu

Introduction

At the end of my Flash seminars, I often overhear students commenting, "Oh, *now* I get it!" Aside from feeling good that I've connected students with an exciting Web development tool, comments like this also remind me that Flash is a lot of fun, but not particularly intuitive.

Flash is a very exciting breakthrough in Web development. But even experienced Web developers will need some help sinking their teeth into creating Flash's vector-graphics based animated, interactive objects, and Web sites. In other words, to create cool Flash movies, even creative folks who have worked with other Web design tools need some help.

This book presents the main features of Flash the same way I've found successful in my seminars. The 22 chapters break Flash down into bite-sized chunks that you can digest from cover to cover, or one-at-a-time as you need them.

Why You Need This Book

Flash is both tremendously fun and seriously complicated. Developing interactive and animated Web sites and Web elements in Flash is often confined to those who are willing to devote themselves to full-time study of the program—unnecessarily.

If you've got the time and inclination to check into a remote monastery and devote yourself full-time to mastering Flash, you might be happier with the thickest Flash book on the bookstore shelf. But if you're a Web developer with a little, some, or quite a bit of Web design experience, this book provides a road map to creating sophisticated Flash movies quickly, fast, and in a hurry.

In the spirit of the *Complete Idiot's Guide* series, I won't assume you're already familiar with any of the technical stuff involved in creating Flash movies. I'll provide clear, complete, and hopefully sometimes humorous explanations and real-world examples so that you have as much fun learning Flash as I have using it.

How to Use This Book

Part 1 of this book (the first two chapters) is something of a "how to use Flash in 25 words or less" introduction to the program. I quickly introduce you to the basic features of Flash, and even show you how to whip together a little movie. Start with those two chapters for a real succinct initiation into Flash.

The heart of the book (Parts 2–6) corresponds to the main elements of Flash: drawing tools (Part 2), layers (Part 3), symbols (Part 4), interactive buttons (Part 5), and animation (Part 6).

Each of these sections is "standalone." You can jump right to buttons, layers, or animation. Or you can follow the sequence of the book. If you have a bit of time (or can *make* a little time), the beginning-to-end approach will probably save you time in the long run by giving you a firm basis to apply the more complex features of Flash near the end of the book.

I've devoted a full section of this book to integrating Flash into other forms of Web pages. Trying to incorporate your wonderful Flash video into an HTML Web page can be like trying to pound a round peg into a square hole, so I've included three chapters that help smooth the edges of that process.

In short, this book has everything you need to create wonderful Web animations quickly with Flash.

Getting the Most Mileage from This Book

You will find that this book does a great job of providing you with all kinds of goodies to help you as you progress through your Flash learning experience. If you are familiar with the *Complete Idiot's Guides*, you should feel right at home as you'll see the usual visual cues and helpers that make things easy to locate and recognize.

If you aren't familiar with this format, here's a quick rundown of what you'll find to speed you on your way:

> ➤ First, you'll notice that **bold text** is used to represent the various menu choices. These are the menus across the very top of your window.

Backstage Pass

One of the cool side elements you'll see as you wind your way through this book is your Backstage Pass. You'll recognize it by that great piece of artwork you see at the top of this box. This is where I'll share some interesting and candid advice about Flash that you might not know or be able to figure out on your own. Don't skip these when you're reading—you don't want to miss out!

> ➤ For those of you who are more keyboard inclined than mouse happy, I've tried to supply some of the more common Flash keyboard shortcuts to make things a little easier for you. The shortcuts are presented for both Macintosh and Windows and

are seen in this order: (Cmd+D) [Ctrl+D] with the Mac being the first set in parentheses and the Windows following in brackets. If you are unfamiliar with using keyboard shortcuts, you might want to try using them occasionally, as they can be real timesavers. Of course, sometimes it seems you may need to use both hands to get the entire set of keys pressed at the same time! For a great resource of helpful Flash keyboard shortcuts, see the Tearcard at the front of the book.

Nitty Gritty Stuff

Now I know you bought a *Complete Idiot's Guide* not because you are a complete idiot, but because you want to learn Flash in a fun, non-techno babble way. However, there are certain technical tidbits that you really need to be aware of to work with Flash effectively. I'll be passing those along to you from time to time alongside the chapter text. When you see the icon above, be sure to hop over and check out the information.

➤ You will recognize new terms because they are seen in *italics* wherever I'm defining the term.

News Flash!

There are certain things that you can't or might not want to do when you're working in Flash. Whenever I need to warn you of something before you move on through the discussion, I'll throw one of these "News Flash!" items at you. Be sure to take note of these as you see them as they could have a profound impact on how your Flash stuff comes out!

Part 1
Flash in a Flash

In the first chapters of this book, you'll learn what Flash does, and how. You will get a basic (not too techie) intro to Flash's memory-efficient way of creating graphics, and how it turns them into animated movies.

You will also learn your way around the Flash environment. You'll set up your working area, and meet the toolbars that will provide you with everything you need to create movies.

HOWS THAT FEEL?

FEEL FEEL FEEL.

COOL!

Chapter 1

Getting a Feel for Flash

In This Chapter

➤ How Flash works

➤ Flash animation

➤ How Flash fits into Web design

➤ What can you do with Flash?

Flash's Place in the World of Web Development

Macromedia Flash 5 allows you to add unique animation and interactivity to Web sites. If you're not familiar with Flash at all, a good place to start might be to jump to the macromedia.com Web site in your browser and follow links to model Flash sites. Or, follow links at my site, www.ppinet.com, to see model Flash projects that closely match things we'll cover in this book.

Instead of static text and graphics—stuff that just sits there—Flash objects add seamless animation and cool interactivity to Web pages. Flash animation means onscreen movies that download quickly, flow smoothly, and look good in any size browser window or monitor. Figure 1.1 catches a frame of a Flash animated home page for my Web site at www.ppinet.com.

Figure 1.1

Without Flash, Web sites just sit there. With Flash—action!

Interactivity means that Web sites *react* to visitors. Display and even site content changes depending on the actions of a viewer. In Figure 1.2, the Up button sends the elevator up.

Figure 1.2

Flash objects add interactivity to Web sites—click a button, and the site content changes.

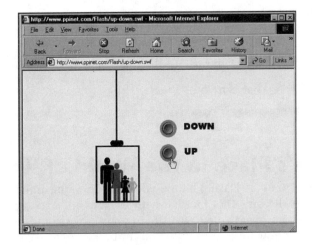

And in Figure 1.3, a Web site is customized for a viewer by adding his name to the site content.

Some of what is accomplished with Flash can be achieved with other technologies, like JavaScript, dynamic HTML, or other movie formats like Macintosh QuickTime. But Flash has two big advantages over other approaches to animation and interactivity: It's easier, and it's more reliable.

Why is that? For most of this book, I'll focus on *how* Flash works. Our goal is to explore and learn Flash in a fun and easy way. But it is helpful to get a quick, basic explanation of what the heck is going on behind the scenes to make Flash so cool, so that's what we'll do in this chapter.

Figure 1.3

In this Flash object, data is entered into the text box and then Flash transfers it into the content of the page.

Let's Do Dessert First!

When I conduct Flash seminars, I always advise my students that creating Flash animations is the easy part of using Flash. The hard work (if you call having fun with Flash "hard work") is to create images in a way that makes them easy to animate.

But my students never really settle down until I let them do an animation. After all, that's the sexy part of Flash, right? So, before we go any farther, I'll walk you through a quick Flash animation. Then we'll step back and walk through all the things required to really control what you're doing.

Nitty Gritty Stuff

Installing Flash

The only requirement for this quick little exercise is that you have installed Flash 5 on your Mac or PC. You can do this by placing the CD in your computer, and accepting all the installation defaults. For more help installing Flash, see "Installing Flash" at the end of this chapter.

So, fasten your seatbelt, and follow these steps to create your first Flash movie:

1. Launch Flash 5. PC users can do this from the Start menu, Mac users from the Flash application folder.

2. When Flash opens, choose **Window**, **Close All Panels** to clear your screen of stuff you haven't learned about yet. Also, pull down the **Window** menu and make sure **Tools** is checked.

3. The window that remains open is the Tool panel. When you hover your mouse over a tool, the tool is identified, as shown in Figure 1.4. Click on the Oval tool (the one shown in the figure).

Figure 1.4

Tools in Flash have shortcut letters—in this figure the Oval tool displays its shortcut letter "O."

The White Space Is the Stage

In Chapter 2, "Getting Around Backstage," I'll properly introduce you to the different elements of the Flash screen. For now, meet the Stage—the white area where you draw pictures.

4. With the Oval tool selected, click and drag to draw an oval in the top right corner of the white area in the middle of the Flash screen, as shown in Figure 1.5.

5. Time to meet a new member of the Flash team—the Timeline. It's the numbered area on top of the Stage. Frames are numbered by fives. Click on Frame number 25, in the Timeline, and press the F6 function key. A dot will appear in Frame 25, as shown in Figure 1.6.

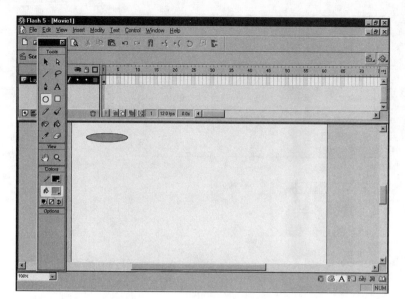

Figure 1.5

Click and drag with the Oval tool to draw a filled oval on the Stage. For now, we'll go with the default colors.

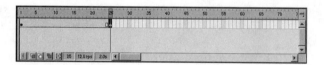

Figure 1.6

Frames with dots in them indicate that those frames have object(s) in them.

6. The Oval is still selected from when you created a new frame—that's why it looks so odd. Click and drag on it to move it to the lower-right corner of the screen, as shown in Figure 1.7.

7. Now comes the interesting part. We'll animate the motion between Frame 1 and Frame 25. To do this, first click in the Timeline in Frame 1. Hold down your Shift key, and click in Frame 25 to select all the frames.

8. Now, with the frames selected, choose **Insert**, **Motion Tween** from the menu. The frames between 1 and 25 turn blue, and an arrow (shown in Figure 1.8) indicates that the motion between Frames 1 and 25 has been animated.

What's Happening?

By selecting Frame 25 and pressing the F6 function key, you copied the oval you drew in Frame 1 into Frame 25. Your two copies of the oval are now separated by 25 blank frames.

Figure 1.7

Moving the copy of the oval in Frame 25 to the bottom right of the Stage.

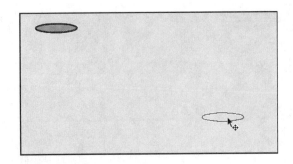

Figure 1.8

Moving your cursor over the frames between 1 and 25 produces a tool tip indicating the frames have been animated with what Flash calls motion tweening.

Backstage Pass

Clearing the Screen

If you want to save your movie, click on the **Save** button in the main toolbar, navigate to a folder, enter a filename, and click on **OK**. Otherwise, just select **File**, **Close** and don't save your movie.

9. You can test your animated movie by pressing the Enter key.

It's that simple! You've created an animated movie. With that as a preview, let's get back on your journey to understand how Flash works. After all, you're probably going to want a little more sophisticated animation than an oval moving from one corner of the stage to another!

How Flash Works

Other programs besides Flash can create animation and interactivity. But Flash is unique in its ability to mesh with the Web.

Flash does this by using two main tools:

➤ Vector-based graphics images to create animation

➤ Action-scripting to create interactivity

These vector-based graphics and scripted movies work because they are viewed with the Flash viewer.

How Flash Animates

Let's break all this down a bit. Flash creates animation (motion) by quickly displaying many *frames* in sequence, as shown in Figure 1.9.

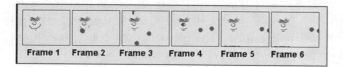

| Frame 1 | Frame 2 | Frame 3 | Frame 4 | Frame 5 | Frame 6 |

Figure 1.9

Flash generates animation by displaying frames like these in sequence.

Like movies shown in a theater with a projector, Flash movies create the illusion of motion by displaying frames quickly (usually about 12 frames per second).

A long movie might be composed of hundreds, even thousands of frames. Using conventional bitmap graphics, those frames would take way too much file space to download into in a browser in our lifetimes—or at least in the attention span of a typical Web viewer.

However, Flash's vector-based graphics, combined with other tricks that you'll explore in this book, keep file sizes far smaller than would be used by bitmap graphics.

The Viewer Makes It All Happen

Both vector graphics and Flash's interactivity—like buttons that send visitors to selected parts of a movie, or to a Web site—work because people view Flash movies using the Flash viewer.

The PR people at Macromedia say that they have a study that shows that 92% of all Web users can view Flash content with their browsers, compared to 84% who can view Java content.

Anyone can download the Flash viewer (also known as the Shockwave viewer) from www.macromedia.com. And it's free! That's because Macromedia wants to sell a lot of copies of Flash, and knows that the more people who have the Flash viewer, the better.

Nitty Gritty Stuff

What About the Other 10% ?

You can design alternate presentations for folks who are using browsers that won't play Flash movies. See Chapter 22, "Exporting Flash Movies" for details.

13

Pixels

Pixels are the tiny dots that make up your computer monitor. If you look closely (not too closely!) at your monitor, you can see that text and graphics are made up of these pixels.

Vector Versus Bitmap Graphics

To appreciate how Flash handles graphics, let's take a quick look at with how *other* Web graphics work. The two universally recognized Web graphic formats, GIF and JPEG, are bitmap graphic formats. A *bitmap* graphic file keeps track of every single pixel in a graphic. The file tracks the color, size, brightness, and location of each of these *pixels*.

Bitmap graphics work okay for displaying a nice photo of the corporate president, or a vista of your rental vacation spa. But they use up too much file size to be used in animation.

Animated GIFs?

An example of using bitmap images as an animation format is animated GIF images. A single GIF file can hold multiple images, and these images can be displayed sequentially, to create a movie effect. Each image that is included in the animated GIF increases the file size, so that a 10-frame animation is likely to take up to 10 times as much file space as a single GIF image. Flash's vector animations are much more efficient.

How Flash Fits into Web Design

Flash's vector-based movies (and all Flash publications are known as "movies") can either be used as standalone Web sites, or can be integrated into an existing Web page.

Figure 1.10 shows three different Flash movies integrated into a Web page that also includes conventional Web page formatting (known as HTML, for HyperText Markup Language).

Or...Flash movies can provide a complete Web interface, like the one shown in Figure 1.11.

Figure 1.10

The three Flash movies include two animations and one interactive form with buttons that react to visitor input. They are embedded in a Web page that includes conventional HTML links and formatted text.

Figure 1.11

Standalone Flash movies like this one are often used as introductions to Web sites.

Fitting Flash movies into HTML Web pages is made easier by Flash's Publish features. We'll walk through that process in detail in Chapter 21, "Putting Flash Online."

What's New in Flash 5?

The biggest and most noticeable change for most of us in Flash 5 is the panel- (or window-) based interface. The new look makes Flash look and act a lot more like its Macromedia cousins FreeHand, Dreamweaver, and Fireworks.

The Flash Interface

We'll explore the Flash interface in detail in Chapter 2, "Getting Around Backstage."

If you've been using earlier versions of Flash, the panels may seem a bit messy at first. But after you've gotten a feel for keeping them under control, you've taken the first step to learning related Macromedia products.

With version 5, Flash beefs up its drawing tool set by adding a Pen tool that draws Bèzier curves.

Who's Bèzier?

Bèzier curves are named after a French engineer/mathematician who invented them, Pierre Bèzier. Bèzier curves are defined by control points. The Pen tool (and Bèzier curves) is covered in Chapter 3, "Ready, Set, Draw!"

Other changes in Flash 5 are more subtle, or are geared to advanced users. The action script language that defines much of Flash's interactivity has changed.

Action Scripts

The changes in Flash's Action Script language are of interest to folks who know JavaScript because the new code is very similar to JavaScript. The rest of us, however, will be generating script by clicking on easy-to-use icons, so changes in the generated code aren't that big a deal to us. We'll check out action scripting in both Chapter 13, "Interacting with the Audience," and Chapter 19, "Advanced Animation Techniques."

Among the other improvements in Flash 5 are support for MP3 audio files, an easier to use color window, and easier to share symbol libraries.

Backstage Pass

Action Scripts

Symbols are an important part of how Flash keeps movie file sizes small. Rather than keep track of separate images in each frame of a movie, repeating *symbol instances* can be altered in different frames. Symbols and symbol instances are the focus of Chapter 10, "Recycling with Symbols."

Installing Flash

As soon as you insert your new Flash 5 CD, the install screen will appear and launch the Flash installation process for your Mac or PC.

You can simply accept all the defaults and install Flash in the folder suggested by Macromedia, with the options most folks want. Do this by clicking **Next** throughout the install process. Or, you can customize installation by utilizing the following options.

Choosing an Install Folder

The first option you'll see in the installation process is a choice of where to install. The default setting will reduce the possibility of required files being misplaced during installation. But if you feel a compelling need to alter the default folder, use the **Browse** button in the Choose Destination Location window of the Install Wizard, and navigate to an alternate folder. Then click **Next**.

Typical, Custom, or Compact?

The Setup Type window in the Install Wizard allows you to choose whether to install the features most Flash users want (Typical), a version of Flash that uses minimal disk space (Compact), or a custom combination of features.

The Typical installation includes the files needed to run the Flash program, Libraries (essentially clip art galleries with graphics and music files), Samples (sample movies), and Lessons (online interactive tutorials for learning Flash).

If you choose Custom, you can select specific features to install. The Custom install screen shown in Figure 1.12 might vary a bit from the final version, but it includes check boxes to install (or not install) the program files, lessons, samples, and library files.

Figure 1.12

This custom installation includes the application files (required to run Flash!) as well as Libraries and Samples. The Lessons are worth installing for interactive assistance with basic Flash tasks.

If you select a compact installation, you won't get Samples or Libraries, but you will still get Lessons.

Installing the Netscape Plug-In

After you tell Flash what you want to install, you'll be prompted to install the Netscape Plug-In. This is the program that allows Flash movies to open seamlessly in Netscape Navigator.

If you want to see your movies in your own Netscape Navigator window, and you have Netscape installed, click **Yes, Install the Plug-in**.

That's it! The Flash installation is quick and easy. If you want to change features later, re-install Flash and make different install selections.

The Least You Need to Know

➤ Flash 5 creates animated and interactive Web site content.

➤ Flash uses vector graphics to save file size, and Action Script to make movies interactive. Only browsers equipped with the Flash viewer can see Flash content.

➤ Macromedia gives away the Flash viewer free at their Web site. Most browsers have the Flash viewer installed.

➤ You can use Flash's Custom Install option to include (or not include) a set of useful interactive lessons.

Chapter 2

Getting Around Backstage

In This Chapter

➤ Meet the Flash environment

➤ Controlling panels

➤ Setting up your movie

➤ Editing frames

➤ Managing what you see

This is the chapter where you take a quick look around the Flash environment. Kind of like a cat in a new home—a sniff here and there just to get a feel for the place.

Much of what you need to know about the Flash environment will be covered as you explore what Flash *does*. So don't spend any time trying to memorize the name of everything on the screen. I'll remind you as we go along.

Meet the Flash Environment

Part of what makes the Flash environment somewhat, shall we say overstocked, is that Flash 5 marks a transition from an older environment to a new one that matches other Macromedia products like Dreamweaver. So, in many cases, there are two or three ways to accomplish something in Flash. Throughout the book, I'll stick with the simplest way to get something done. In this chapter, however, I'll introduce you to alternate ways to organize your Flash environment so you are aware of what is available and can set things up in the way most convenient for your work methods.

If you're familiar with file menus, toolbars, and tools in a Macintosh/Windows environment, the Flash menu and toolbar will look familiar to you. But Flash has it's own unique elements as well.

When you launch Flash 5, a new movie opens. The big white area in the middle of the screen is called the *Stage* (get it—a movie analogy). The rows on top (Layer 1) are called *Layers*. And the small rectangles with numbers at 1, 5, 10, 15, and so on are *frames*. The strip that holds frames is called the *Timeline*. Flash 5 has added a *status bar* in the lower left corner of the Flash window.

That's pretty much the Flash environment. Figure 2.1 shows the Flash environment with key elements identified.

Figure 2.1

An empty stage, ready for a movie

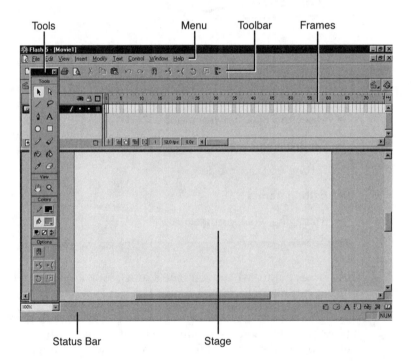

You do all your drawing on the Stage. The Timeline controls animation, and Layers allow you to stack images on top of one another, while editing them one at a time.

Toolbar Versus Tools

You can do a majority of what needs to be done in Flash by choosing features from the *toolbar* at the top of the Flash window, or the Toolbox. The Toolbox is normally docked at the left side of your screen, but you can drag on the word "Tools" and move the window anywhere on your screen.

The options in the toolbar and the Toolbox duplicate features that can be accessed from the File menu. Which is a better way to choose features? In general, you'll save time and focus better on your movie by relying on tools in the toolbar and Toolbox when they are available, as opposed to hunting around for file options.

Have a Seat at the Tool Bar

Tools? Toolbar? They sound similar. Let's start with the main toolbar. It has standard Macintosh/Windows tools like Save and Print. Figure 2.2 identifies the tools in the Flash toolbar. New, Open, Save, Print, and so on are typical to most Macintosh/Windows applications.

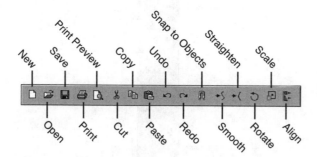

Figure 2.2

The Flash toolbar—not to be confused with the Flash tools.

The standard toolbar also includes some unique Flash icons. The *Snap to Objects* button toggles attraction between objects to one another (as if they were magnetized). The *Smooth* and *Straighten* tools change the way you edit lines—a feature you'll explore in Chapter 3, "Ready, Set, Draw!"

The *Rotate* tool adds rotation handles to a selected object so you can rotate it, and the *Scale* tool allows you to resize objects interactively. The *Alignment* tool allows you to arrange objects in relation to one another. Alignment, resizing and scaling are explained in Chapter 6, "Snip, Snap, Stick."

Float with the Toolbox

The Toolbox is different from the toolbar. The Toolbox can be displayed or hidden by choosing **Window**, **Tools** from the menu bar.

Backstage Pass

A Bit Redundant

All the tools in the toolbar duplicate functions that can be accomplished with selections from the menu bar.

The Toolbox stores valuable Flash icons that allow you to create and control illustrations you create in Flash.

Figure 2.3 identifies each tool in the Toolbox.

Figure 2.3

The Flash Toolbox stores drawing tools and tools for controlling drawings. As different tools are selected, different options become available in the Options area of the Toolbox.

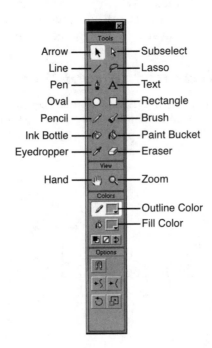

In the course of this book, you'll learn to use all these tools. Here, I'll briefly describe them:

- ➤ The **Arrow** tool selects objects (shapes and lines).
- ➤ The **Subselect** tool reveals individual editing nodes within objects.
- ➤ The **Line** tool draws lines.
- ➤ The **Lasso** tool selects irregular shaped groups of objects.
- ➤ The **Pen** tool draws Bèzier curves by defining nodal points for a curve.
- ➤ The **Text** tool allows you to create blocks of text.
- ➤ The **Oval** tool draws circles and ovals.
- ➤ The **Rectangle** tool draws squares and rectangles.
- ➤ The **Pencil** draws curved or angled lines.
- ➤ The **Brush** draws broad swipes on the screen.
- ➤ The **Ink** bottle assigns colors to lines.
- ➤ The **Paint** bucket assigns colors to fills.

➤ The **Eyedropper** transfers colors from one line or fill to another line or fill.

➤ The **Eraser** deletes areas of a drawing.

➤ The **Hand** tool allows you to click and drag to move a drawing around your window.

➤ The **Zoom** tool zooms in or out to magnify or telescope sections of your drawing.

➤ The **Stroke Color** swatch allows you to select an outline color for selected objects.

➤ The **Fill Color** swatch allows you to select a fill color for selected objects.

➤ **Default colors** changes selected stroke and fill colors to the movie default.

➤ **No color** removes either the fill or the stroke color from a drawing.

➤ **Swap colors** transfers the stroke color to the fill color and vice versa.

Making Movies

As soon as you launch Flash, a new movie opens. You are ready to start designing your movie. And of course when you are done with the movie you'll want to save your fabulous creation by choosing **File**, **Save**.

Backstage Pass

Movie1...Movie2...

You can have more than one Flash movie open at a time—just choose **File**, **New** from the menu. As you create new movies, Flash names them Movie1, Movie2, and so on. When you save a movie, you can assign a more creative and descriptive file name. The Window menu allows you to choose between open movies.

The main work area of Flash is divided into two regions—the Stage is the wide open space that takes up most of the Flash window. Here's where you add the content that will show up in your movie.

Movies are almost always made up of many *frames*. Animation is produced by displaying those frames in succession—usually at a rate of 12 frames per second if the movie is to be displayed on a Web site. If a movie is for a CD or other non-Web media, then a frame rate of 24 or 30 fps is often used.

Interactivity Comes from Frames

Here's a concept to trip on as you learn your way around the Flash environment: Not only is Flash animation created by using frames, but so is *interactivity*. For example, you might program a movie so visitors push buttons to choose the content of their movie. The basic action that is performed by these buttons (behind the scenes) is to jump a viewer to a section of frames within the movie. You'll explore this in detail in Chapter 19, "Advanced Animation Techniques."

Get on Stage

To create objects in a Flash frame, you add them to the Stage. If you aren't the artistic type, you can copy objects from other programs onto the Stage or you can import files created outside of Flash onto the Stage. However, because Flash is such an easy to use program, you can also create new drawings on the Stage yourself. Much of this book is about how to do just that.

For now, just note that objects that are *off* the Stage (the white area of the workspace), like the folks in the elevator in Figure 2.4, will not appear in a movie.

Figure 2.4

Often objects are placed off the stage in one frame of a movie, only to move onto the stage in later frames—much like an actor "waiting in the wings" for his or her entrance onto a real stage.

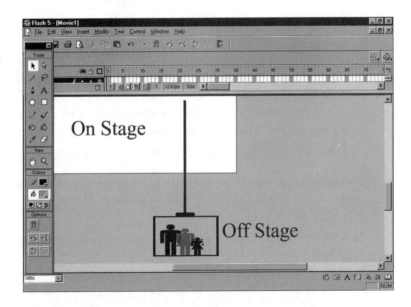

Frames and the Timeline

The Timeline, located just above the Stage, displays a series of numbered frames. Frames are numbered by fives—5, 10, 15, 20, and so on.

You select a frame by clicking on it in the Timeline.

If you want to edit a frame, you convert it into a *keyframe*. Choosing **Insert**, **Keyframe** creates an editable frame that duplicates the previously selected frame. Choosing **Insert**, **Blank Keyframe** creates a frame that can be edited, but doesn't have anything in it.

Nitty Gritty Stuff

Frames...and Keyframes

As you will see, most frames in a movie have content but *you don't edit them*. That's because the content of most animated frames is *generated by Flash* as it automates the process of animating action. We'll dig into this in detail when we explore animation in Chapter 15, "Everybody Dance Now!"

Keyframes are marked with a dot in the timeline. Changes to objects are always associated with a keyframe.

If you select a frame and do not create a keyframe on that frame, and you modify objects on the stage that are linked with that layer, then the keyframe to the left of the selected frame gets modified.

There is a set of icons under the Timeline that is used for viewing multiple frames at once. We won't go into the details of those now, but just know that they are useful when creating animations. You'll use these icons in Chapter 16, "Automating Animation."

The Layered Look

Notice that the Timeline is composed not only of frames, but also of layers. Layers allow you to stack objects on top of one another within a frame. For example, one layer might contain a background, a second layer might contain action figures, and a third layer might be used to hold sound files.

Layers Are Optional

Although you CAN create movies using only one layer, you can do a more efficient job and make later editing easier by using multiple layers.

Layers are a powerful feature for managing Flash movies, and we'll get into them in detail in Chapter 8, "Working with Layers."

Controlling Panels

The biggest makeover in Flash 5 is the incorporation of the same Control Panel environment used in other Macromedia products, including Dreamweaver.

Panels provide a set of options for selected objects. You can view a panel by choosing **Window**, **Panel** from the menu, and then selecting one of the 17 different available panels, as shown in Figure 2.5.

Figure 2.5

The Windows, Panel sub-menu offers panels for commonly used features like Mixer—that defines colors—or advanced (and somewhat obscure) features like Clip Parameters that is only active when you generate a mini-movie called a Movie Clip.

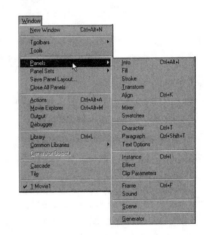

Docked Panels

Most panels are displayed as docked panels. For example, the Info panel in Figure 2.6 is docked with three other panels that display different information and controls.

Figure 2.6

The Info panel is docked with the Transform, Stroke, and Fill panels. You can select any of these panels by clicking on a tab. Or, you can click and drag on a panel tab to detach it from other panels.

Panels and Objects

Panels display information about, or apply changes to, selected objects. If, for example, you are working with a bunch of objects, you can select them all, and use the Mixer panel to apply changes to all the selected objects.

In Figure 2.7, the color selected in the Mixer panel is applied to the selected oval, but not the two ovals that are not selected.

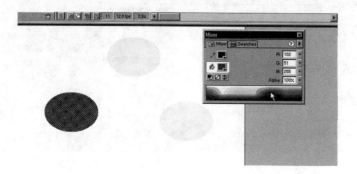

Figure 2.7

Only the selected (dark) object is going through a color change as a new color is selected from the Mixer panel.

Managing Panels

Panels can provide incredible control over your drawings, but they can also get in the way and clutter up your screen. Figure 2.8 shows a window almost obscured by panels.

To help you control panels, Flash 5 allows you to save sets of panels. To do this, open the panels you want to use, and then choose **Window**, **Save Panel Layout**. The Save Panel Layout dialog box appears, as shown in Figure 2.9.

Backstage Pass

Why Doesn't My Panel Do Anything?

Sometimes, Panels display nothing at all. For example, if you have a big red oval selected and you activate the Text panel, you won't see any information about your oval because the Text panel only controls and provides information about text—and there isn't any in a plain ol' oval.

Figure 2.8

Yikes! This over-stuffed Flash screen is crammed with open Panels—the four little windows that fill the right side of the screen. For those of us who like a cleaner workspace, you can either up your screen resolution, or else restrict yourself to no more than a panel or two at a time.

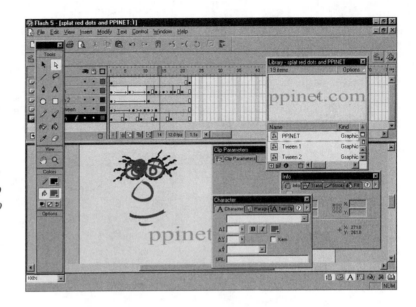

Figure 2.9

Save your favorite groups of panels as saved layouts. Saved layouts are available in any movie you create. To open a saved panel layout, choose **Window**, **Panel Sets**, *and click on a saved panel.*

Using the Status Bar to View Panels

There are seven icons (not to be confused with the seven dwarfs, or false icons!) in the status bar that hang out in the lower-right corner of the Flash window. They activate (or hide) some of the more popular panels (as judged by a *panel* of experts!).

Those icons are illustrated in Figure 2.10.

Because we'll be exploring many panels in the course of this book, and because all 17 panels have multiple tabs and many options within each tab, we'll just briefly describe the panels here:

➤ **Info**—Control size and color—the basics.

➤ **Fill**—Controls the fill color of a selected object.

➤ **Stroke**—Controls the outline of a selected object.

➤ **Transform**—Rotates, resizes, and skews selected objects.

➤ **Align**—Lines up selected objects in relation to one another.

➤ **Mixer** and **Swatches**—Two tabs of the same panel that select colors.

➤ **Character**, **Paragraph**, and **Text**—Three tabs of the same panel that control how text looks, and what special properties are assigned to text boxes.

➤ **Instance**, **Effect**, **Frame**, and **Sound**—Four tabs of the same panel. The **Instance** and **Effect** tabs control how Flash displays symbols that are repeatedly used. The Frame tab controls animation, and the Sound tab controls sounds associated with a movie.

➤ **Scene**—Organizes large movies that are broken down into smaller scenes.

➤ **Generator**—Special features to generate Web sites from movies.

Show/Hide

Character — Movie Explorer

Info — 🗇 ❸ A 🗂 ❧ 🎵 🕮 — Library
NUM

Mixer ⌐ Instance ⌐ Object Actions

Zoom

100% ▾

Figure 2.10

The icons in the Status Bar toggle between opening and closing frequently used panels. The drop-down menu on the left side of the status bar allows you to zoom in and out of a drawing.

Now you know what all the Panels do. Use 'em, or ignore 'em. But keep in mind that everything you can do with a panel, you can also do with a menu option.

Changing Movie Properties

There are some elements of a movie that apply to a *whole* movie—like background color, stage size, and frame rate.

You can define the background color for a movie by choosing **Modify**, **Movie**, and clicking on a color in the Background Color palette in the Modify Movie dialog box (see Figure 2.11).

Change the size of the Stage by changing the dimensions in the Width and Height boxes of the Modify Movie dialog box.

Backstage Pass

What If You Want to Change These Things During a Movie?

The short answer is that you string together multiple movies. The long answer is found in Chapter 17, "Keeping It All Together."

Figure 2.11

Changes made in the Modify Movie dialog box apply to the entire movie.

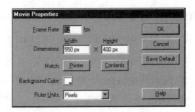

You can speed up a movie by increasing the frame rate in the Frame Rate box. Slow the movie down by decreasing the frame rate.

Jerky Versus Smooth Animation

The frame rate changes the speed the movie plays, but it also determines how choppy or how smoothly the animation will be. If I create my movie at 30 fps and use 30 frames to represent one second of action the action will take 1 second, but will be smoother than if I created 12 frames at 12 fps.

The Powerful Preferences Box

You can define the way Flash works by making changes in the Preferences dialog box. This little dialog box is pretty powerful—one might almost say you can add your own flash to Flash by making changes in it.

Some of the preference settings may not mean much until you explore the actual features of Flash. But you should at least be aware of the kinds of controls available here.

Open the Preferences dialog box by choosing **Edit, Preferences** (see Figure 2.12).

How Flash Works—In General

The General tab controls basic Flash functions—it's shown in Figure 2.12.

➤ The **Undo Levels** field defines how many times you can click on the Undo button to reverse your previous actions.

➤ The **Disable PostScript** check box cancels out PostScript printing. This option is not available on Macintosh computers.

➤ The **Shift Select** check box enables holding down the Shift key while clicking with the Arrow (or any selection) tool to select multiple objects.

➤ The **Show Tooltips** check box makes those handy little explanations appear when you hover over a button—why turn this off?

➤ The **Disable Timeline Docking** check box makes it hard to stick the Timeline at the top of the Flash screen. Pass on this one.

➤ The **Flash 4 Selection Style** check box allows you to select frames in the Timeline the way you did it back in the olden days of Flash 4. Accustomed to Flash 4? Then this option might save some aggravation but keep in mind that directions in this book will be for the Flash 5 selection method.

➤ The **Flash 4 Frame Drawing** check box displays those cute little hollow circles in blank keyframes the way Flash 4 used to do it.

➤ The **Highlight Color** area enables you to control how selected objects are displayed.

➤ The **Mode** drop-down list in the Actions Panel area of the dialog box allows you to choose between Normal Mode, and Expert Mode. The default, Normal mode, displays a handy list of Basic actions when you start adding interactive programming to your movie. The Expert mode option does not display that useful list.

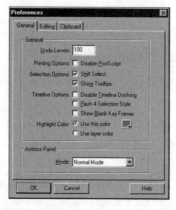

Figure 2.12

*The Preferences dialog box with the **General** tab selected.*

Define How Flash Edits and Copies

The **Editing** tab of the Preferences dialog box defines how objects are selected and displayed for editing. Even though you've not started doing any drawing or editing at this point, you need to be aware of the options available for changing your editing preferences. Then when you run across something that doesn't work for you, you'll know if it's possible to change it and where to look.

The Editing tab is shown in Figure 13.

Figure 2.13

Drawing settings define how much help you want from Flash in connecting lines, or smoothing curves.

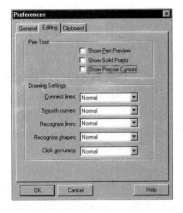

The Pen tool check boxes control how Bézier curves are drawn—if you choose the **Show Pen Preview** option, you'll see curves as you draw them. The **Show Solid Points** check box will display nodal points within a curve, and the **Show Precise Cursors** check box changes the cursor to a crosshair when drawing bezier curves.

The **Drawing** settings define how lines you draw get converted to shapes and curves.

The **Clipboard** tab of the Preferences dialog box defines how objects are copied into the Clipboard. This is useful if you plan to copy a lot of objects from Flash into other programs.

The Least You Need to Know

➤ The Flash environment will look familiar to you if you've used a Macintosh or Windows machine before.

➤ The Flash toolbar is normally docked at the top of the screen. The Flash Toolbox, normally docked at the left side of the screen, provides access to drawing tools.

➤ Flash allows access to almost all its features either through menus or through panels. It's kind of a left brain/right brain thing. If you like the graphical interface of panels, and you have a nice 32" 1280×1024 resolution monitor, you can display several panels and still have workspace visible on your monitor. Or, you can work with a nice clean screen, and rely on the menu for everything you need out of Flash.

➤ The Flash environment is highly customizable—use Edit Preferences to change how Flash works, how shapes and curves are drawn and edited, or how Flash copies objects to the Clipboard. Or, just leave the preferences alone and work with the Flash defaults.

Part 2
Lights! Camera! Vectors????

Flash comes with a professional set of drawing tools to create cool Web graphics, and to organize the shapes, lines, and fills that will someday be actors in your Flash movie.

In the following chapters, you will learn to create and edit drawings in Flash. Drawing talent not required.

Chapter 3

Ready, Set, Draw!

In This Chapter

➤ Drawing lines

➤ Changing how lines look

➤ Curves and zigzag lines

➤ Drawing Bèzier curves

➤ Creating ovals and rectangles

Drawing lines and shapes for your Flash movie is kind of like hiring actors for a regular movie. Except that you get to *create* these actors.

Much of the content of your animated movie will consist of moving shapes, lines, and text. In this chapter, you'll learn to use Flash's line and shape tools to create and manipulate the objects that will be flying around Web sites to present your message.

Let's break down exactly how to use the stroke (line) and shape tools in Flash.

Backstage Pass

Lines? Or Strokes?

Flash calls 'em strokes; most of us call 'em lines. Well, different strokes for different folks, as Sly and the Family Stone used to sing. I'll call them both strokes and lines in this section just to keep everyone happy.

Get It Straight

Two bits of advice on drawing lines in Flash:

➤ Drawing in Flash is fun, whether you can draw or not.

➤ Flash gives you a LOT of help!

If you're a talented sketch artist (like my artist, Paul), you'll find Flash's drawing tools give you the freedom to create some really cool stuff. If you're a drawing klutz (like me), you can still have a lot of fun, and Flash will help cover up your lack of drawing skill by rounding, smoothing, straightening, and adding effects to your drawings.

Backstage Pass

Where Do Drawings Come From?

Fact is, most artists don't create complex drawings in Flash. Instead, really complex illustrations are often created by modifying images from Flash's Library or other sources. The Flash Drawing tools are often used for basic drawings, shapes, and enhancing imported artwork.

Flash provides two main ways to draw lines—the Line tool and the Pencil tool. You can choose them from the Drawing toolbar (on the left of the Stage), or you can pick the Pencil tool by pressing P on the keyboard, and the Line tool by pressing N on the Toolbox.

Figure 3.1

Before you begin to draw with lines in Flash, you'll want to define line options like line color, width and type. These options are set in the Options area that appears at the bottom of the toolbar when you select the Line or Pencil tools.

Line tool —
Pen tool —

Pencil tool —

The Line, Pen, and Pencil tools allow you to use options to change line color, thickness and style. The Pencil tool also allows you to modify how you want curves handled, but we'll get that a little later in the chapter.

Setting Stroke Color

Clicking on the Stroke Color button in the Color area of the Toolbox opens a palette of colors. The color you choose defines the color for strokes you draw with the Pencil, Line, and Pen tools option. From now on, any line you draw will appear with that color.

That Pen Tool

Later in this chapter we'll explore a third way to draw special curves using the Pen tool. It's a bit tricky and specialized, so we'll focus on lines first.

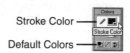

Stroke Color

Default Colors

Figure 3.2

You can modify the stroke colorfor lines in the Colors area of the Toolbox. Default color settings draw a black line.

Figure 3.3

Picking a color for a line from the color palette.

Don't like any of the colors in the color palette? You can mix up your own color by clicking on the Color wheel button in the upper right corner of the Color Palette. This opens the Color dialog box. The Solid tab of the dialog box allows you to define colors not available from the default Flash color palette. You can mix up a custom color by entering values in the R (Red), G (Green), B (Blue) fields. Or you can choose a color from the Color space on the right side of the dialog box.

We'll examine colors in more detail in Chapter 5.

Pick Line Color First

Can you change the color of a line after you draw it? Yes, and we'll explore that process in Chapter 5, when we look at assigning fill colors. But for now all you need to know is that it's easier to assign a line color before you draw. One reason for that is that lines you draw in Flash are often converted to more than one line after they're drawn, meaning that you have to recolor several different line objects. In short, it usually helps to figure out your line color in advance.

Browser-Safe Colors

The default set of colors in Flash are "browser safe," meaning that they are compatible with the colors which Web browsers like Netscape Navigator and Internet Explorer can interpret. We'll explore color palettes and browser-safe colors in more detail in "Protecting Your Colors," Chapter 5. For now, it's a good idea to just stick with the default palette—if you want the colors you choose in Flash to show up precisely in a Web browser.

Setting Stroke Thickness and Style

The option Stroke Panel allows you to choose line style, line thickness, and line color. Choose **Window**, **Panels**, **Stroke** to open the Stroke Panel.

Use the Stroke Style drop-down list to choose from a nice variety of line types. Use the Stroke Height slider (as shown in Figure 3.4) to choose a line thickness (or type a value in the box).

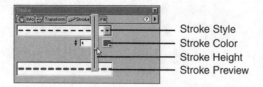

Figure 3.4

Changing line thickness with the Stroke slider. As you define stroke (line) height, style and color, the Preview area of the Stroke panel shows you how your line will appear.

Stroke Style
Stroke Color
Stroke Height
Stroke Preview

Thick or Thin? It's Up to You!

Custom lines are great because they give you more control over your drawings by allowing you to set the line thickness to whatever you want—within parameters. Line thicknesses are defined in points. There are 72 points per inch. Line thicknesses can range from .10 points to 10 points, and can be set as precisely as a one-hundredth of a point.

The Stroke Panel also provides an alternate way to choose stroke color—you can click on the Stroke Color swatch to open the color palette and choose a new line color.

Lines with Custom Style

The Stroke Style option drop-down list in the Stroke panel allows you to choose from pre-set line styles. The preset options—hairline, solid, dashed, dotted, ragged, stippled, and hatched—are illustrated when you click on the dropdown list, as shown in Figure 3.5.

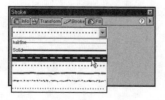

Figure 3.5

You can choose from pre-set line styles—or define your own.

For more detailed control over line style (and more fun), choose Custom from the flyout menu on the right of the Stroke panel, as shown in Figure 3.6.

Figure 3.6

Choosing the Custom option for Stroke style.

When you define a custom stroke style in the Line Style dialog box, you get a whole bunch of detailed options that you can use to define the line style.

Backstage Pass

Stroke Style Controversy

There's controversy in the Flash community over whether wild stroke styles work well in Web sites. Some experts say getting tricky with line styles is a no-no, and that the subtlety of line styles get lost by the time they arrive in a Web browser. Maybe so, but there is definitely a time and place for some cool line styles—especially with large, not too detailed graphics like the ones Paul contributed in Figure 3.7.

In Figure 3.7, Paul has gone to town with line styles. For the figure on the left, he tweaked the Stipple line style by assigning

➤ Dot Size: Large

➤ Dot Variation: Random

➤ Density: Very Sparse

➤ 4pt with sharp corners

For the figure on the right, Paul used the Simple pattern, and selected these options in the Line Style dialog box:

➤ Wave Height: Wild

➤ Wave Length: Very Short

➤ 4pt with sharp corners

Figure 3.7
You can fine tune different attributes of the Stroke styles.

Drawing Straight Lines and Angles

After you define your stroke color, thickness, and style, it's time to draw! If you're drawing with the Line tool, your lines are gonna be straight, no matter how shaky your drawing hand.

With the Line tool selected, just click and drag to draw a line. Only when you *release* the mouse button does the line actually appear.

Backstage Pass

Drawing Angles

As you draw a line, you'll notice a magnetic pull to draw your line at a 90° angle—up, down, right, or left. That's handy, unless you want to draw a line that is *almost* straight up and down (or sideways), but not completely. In that case, from the **View** menu, deselect the default **Snap on** setting, and your lines will no longer "snap" to 90° angles. Even with Snap turned off, holding down the Shift key as you draw constrains your lines to 45° angles.

Throw Me a Curve

The Line tool works for straight lines, but when you want to draw illustrations, curves or zigzags, turn to the Pencil tool.

When you select the Pencil tool (remember the shortcut—just press "Y"), a new Option appears that isn't available for the Line tool. The Pencil Mode option allows you to choose between Straighten, Smooth, or Ink. These tools don't do exactly what you might expect—for instance, the "Straighten" tool is great for drawing...circles! And the Ink tool can be combined with either straightening or smoothing.

Figure 3.8

Drawing something close to a circle in Straighten mode ends up a perfect circle.

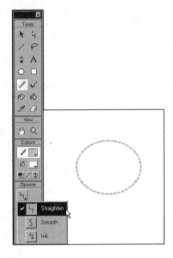

Straight Line Zigzags

Contrary to what the name implies, the Straighten option does not necessarily create straight lines. Yes, when you select Straighten from the Pencil Mode option button, Flash will convert your lines into relatively symmetrical zig-zags. And a slightly-wandering line becomes straight. But Straighten also converts curves to symmetrical, smooth shapes. For example, an unsteady zig-zag becomes a neat angle. And an ungainly, poorly drawn egg becomes a smooth oval.

Drawing Smooth Curves

The Smooth option removes little distortions from lines, and transforms them into smooth curves.

From Curve to Straighten—or Vice Versa

You can transform a line from curved to straightened, or vice versa. Do this by drawing a marquee around the curve with the Select tool, and then choosing Modify, Smooth or Modify, Straighten to change the properties of an existing curve.

Nitty Gritty Stuff

How Does Flash Do It?

Flash converts your poorly drawn lines (OK, *my* poorly drawn lines) into smooth, or symmetrical curves and angles by applying some math. Remember our discussion in chapter one about how Flash uses mathematical calculations to define lines—a process known as *vector* graphics. These mathematical calculations are *altered* a bit as you draw, to help smooth and sharpen your lines.

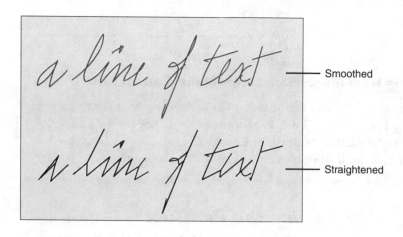

Smoothed

Straightened

Figure 3.9
This hand-drawn text was modified from smooth mode to straighten mode.

Getting More Help...Or Less

If you want to apply more dramatic changes to your curves, choose **Edit Preferences** from the menu and in the Editing tab, change the Smooth Curves setting in the dialog box to Smooth (see Figure 3.10). Want less help? Change the setting to Rough. Don't like getting help at all with your curves? Choose Off from the Smooth Curves drop-down menu in the Assistant dialog box.

Open and Closed Curves

Flash will assist you in connecting lines. If you use the Pencil tool with the Straighten option, you can draw *almost* connecting lines, and Flash will connect them.

Figure 3.10

You can enhance or disable Flash's ability to help straighten or smooth your curves.

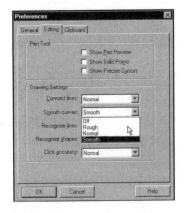

Changing How Much Flash Helps Make Connections

To adjust the amount of help you get from Flash in connecting lines (or to turn off all help connecting lines), choose **Edit**, **Preferences**, and click on the Editing tab. You will see Must Be Close, Normal, or Can Be Distant. Can Be Distant will force your lines to connect if you only come close to connecting them.

Who is Bèzier?

Pierre Bèzier was a French automobile designer who developed a method for generating curves by defining "control points" that regulate the curves.

Using the Pen Tool

The Pen tool is used to generate smooth, synchronized curves called Bèzier curves.

The best way to "explain" the Pen tool is to illustrate it with an example. Everyone have their pens out?

To generate a wave-like curve with the Pen tool, draw a vertical line from top to bottom on the left side of the stage. With this first step, you are defining control points for one end of the curve.

Next, click on the right side of the stage, and draw another vertical line, again starting from top of the stage and drawing down. As you do, you will generate a curve between the two control points you defined, as shown in Figure 3.11.

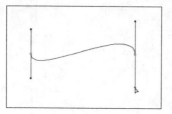

Figure 3.11

The Pen tool is used to define control points that generate curves.

Backstage Pass

Making Waves

Generating curves with the Pen tool can be a bit unpredictable. My trick is to draw something *close* to the curve I want, and then modify the lines. And modifying drawn lines just happens to be the next section of this chapter! So read on....

Modifying Drawn Lines

To change the direction, shape or length of an *existing* line, use the Select tool. When you click on the *end* of an existing line, the Select tool displays as a right angle. Click and drag to move the end of a line. As you begin to drag the end of the line, the cursor displays as a circle, as shown in Figure 3.12.

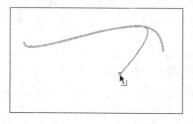

Figure 3.12

Use the Select tool, not the Pencil, Pen, or Line tool, to modify an existing line.

If you use the Select tool to click in the *middle* (not the end) of an existing line, the cursor displays as a curve icon. Click and drag with this icon to change the *curve* of a selected line, as shown in Figure 3.13.

47

Figure 3.13

Click and drag on the middle of an existing line with the Select tool to change curves.

Stepping Out of the Box

The Oval and Rectangle tools can be used to draw shapes that include an outline, or shapes without an outline. Can't you draw ovals and rectangles with the Line or Pencil tools? Sure you can, but the Oval and Rectangle tools are shortcuts that help you draw those shapes in a hurry.

News Flash

Nothin' + Nothin' = Nothin'

Beware of turning off *both* outlining and fill color. If you do that, your shape will have neither an outline, nor a fill. In other words, you won't draw *anything*.

Backstage Pass

Drawing Circles

To draw a prefect circle, hold down the Shift key as you draw an oval.

Drawing Ovals

To draw an oval, just select the Oval tool from the toolbar (or just press "O" on your keyboard). When you click on the Stroke Color option in the Toolbox, you open the familiar color palette. The color you select here determines which color gets assigned to the *outline* of your oval. Don't want *any* outline? Then click first on the Stroke Color icon in the Toolbox, and then click the No Color options icon to turn off outlining, as shown in Figure 3.14.

The Fill panel Color icon in the Toolbox opens a color palette that lets you choose a color for the *inside* of your oval. If you want an oval with *no* fill, choose the Fill options icon in the option area of the Toolbox, and click the No Color icon.

Once you've defined your oval's outline and fill, click and draw away to create ovals.

Drawing Rectangles

Drawing rectangles is similar to drawing ovals—first you define the color, thickness, and style of the outline and the fill color, then you click and draw. Holding down the Shift key as you draw creates a perfect square.

Figure 3.14

Choosing No Color with the Stroke Color option selected turns off outlining for your oval so only the color you choose for the inside of the shape will show.

Snap to Squares

If you have Snap turned on (from the View menu, see if Snap To Objects is selected), rectangles will tend to "snap to" being a square if you draw one that is even close to being a square. If that gets in your way, disable snap while you draw your rectangles.

The Rectangle tool has an option that you won't find in the Oval toolbar—the Round Rectangle Radius option. Radius settings range from 0 (none), to 999 (very curved).

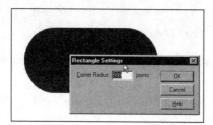

Figure 3.15

A radius of 999 creates very rounded corners turning the rectangle into more of a oval type shape, while a radius of 1 gently softens the corners leaving the shape more recognizable as a rectangle.

When Shapes and Lines Intersect

In Flash, when shapes or lines intersect, new objects are created. In most drawing programs, a line stays *one line* even if it is intersected by another line. With Flash, an intersected line becomes *two lines*. Shapes work the same way.

Once you get the hang of working with intersecting lines and shapes, you'll use intersection as a cool drawing technique.

Figure 3.16

Moving one filled object over another and then moving the object away leaves a cut in the original. To make the separations in the arms and legs of the character, simply highlight the forearm section and drag it away.

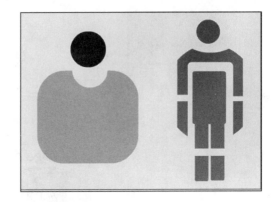

Backstage Pass

Looking Ahead to Layers

Don't want intersecting objects to cut each other up? The way around this is to place intersecting objects in different Layers. Check out Chapter 8, "Working with Layers," for the lowdown on layers.

The Least You Need to Know

You can apply formatting to change the size, font, color, and paragraph properties of text.

➤ The Line, Oval, Rectangle, Pen, and Pencil tools are used to draw lines, curves, and shapes.

➤ Each line and shape tool has its option buttons in the Toolbox that allow you to set the line (and fill) color *before* you start drawing.

➤ The Pencil tool is the most flexible way to create drawings in Flash. The Pencil Mode option let's you either straighten or smooth curves.

➤ When you drag a shape or line on top of another shape or line, you *cut* the second shape. Sometimes this produces two dissected lines; sometimes it produces a shape with a piece "cut out."

Chapter 4

Paint the Town

In This Chapter

➤ Using brush tools to create cool, artsy strokes

➤ Weaving brush strokes in front of and behind existing objects

➤ Cleaning up drawings with the Eraser tool

➤ Using the Eraser as a drawing tool

There's more to Flash's Brushes and the Eraser than you might expect. You can use brushes to simulate the appearance of fountain pens or broad paint strokes, but you can also use options that turn Brushes and Erasers into tools that weave in and out of existing objects, selectively applying their magic.

Brushin' Up

Flash's brush tool works like a real paint brush, or a fountain pen. By varying the brush you select, and the way you paint, you can create some very nice effects.

The brush tool has options that change the Fill Color, Size, and Shape of your brush (see Figure 4.1). It also has a Brush Mode tool, which is really one of the cooler drawing tools you'll find.

Grab the Brush tool by pressing **B** on your keyboard or clicking its icon in the toolbox.

Figure 4.1

The brush color is deter-mined by the color you select from the Fill Color Palette. The Brush tool options allow you to change the color, size, and shape of a brush.

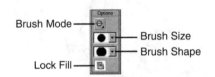

Brush Mode

Brush Size

Brush Shape

Lock Fill

Backstage Pass

Other Options

The Brush Mode option changes the way that brush strokes interact with other objects on your page. We'll get to that a bit later in this chapter because this is such a powerful feature it deserves some space of it's own.

If you have a drawing tablet connected to your computer, yet another option appears—the Use Pressure icon. Selecting this option lets your drawing tablet work like a fountain pen or a paintbrush dripping with paint. The harder you press, the more "ink" will flow.

Selecting Brushes

To assign a brush color, click on the **Fill Color** option, and choose a color from the palette. If you read Chapter 3 on drawing, there's nothin' too new here, but brush sizes and shapes are what make the tool unique.

Choose a brush size by clicking the **Brush Size** tool, and selecting one of the ten available brush sizes from the pop-up menu (see Figure 4.2).

Figure 4.2

Brushes come in ten sizes—which can be made even bigger if you paint with Zoom set at something smaller than 100%.

Backstage Pass

Need BIGGER (or Smaller) Brushes?

What, ten brush sizes aren't enough for you? You can effectively enlarge the size of a brush by changing the Zoom percentage from the Standard Toolbar. The widest paintbrush setting becomes twice as wide when painted on a screen displayed at 50% zoom. And, for that matter, the tiniest brush size gets half as big when painted on a screen enlarged to 200%. But you're likely to find the available brushes cover pretty much anything you need at 100%.

The nine brush shapes shown in Figure 4.3 let you control how paint gets splashed on the screen.

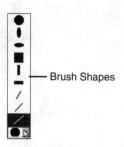

— Brush Shapes

Figure 4.3

Brush Shapes

Irregular (not round or square) brush shapes act differently when dragged in different directions—just like a wide paintbrush behaves when you slide it sideways or stroke it up and down. Figure 4.4 shows an illustration using different brush shapes.

Figure 4.4

The slashing "z" effect that gives the look of a pine tree in this drawing is created by using a horizontal brush shape.

Creating Cool Brush Effects

The really interesting stuff with brushes happens when you start messing around with the five available brush modes. Click the Brush Mode option in the Brush toolbox to see the options (see Figure 4.5).

Figure 4.5

You can use brushes to paint over, on top of, or behind another object.

The Normal brush mode just paints over everything in its path. Paint Fills mode turns your paintbrush into a tool that only paints on fills, not lines. The Paint Behind setting applies brush strokes only behind an existing object.

Figure 4.6

Different brush strokes affect drawings in different ways.

The Paint Selection brush mode applies brush strokes to a selected object. Paint Inside mode is somewhat deceptively named. It applies brush strokes only to the area in which you start painting. If you start painting on the stage outside of any object, you actually paint *outside* the objects. But if you start painting on an object, the paint only applies to that object (see Figure 4.7).

Figure 4.7

In the drawing on the left, the face was selected before painting in Paint Selection mode. In the drawing on the right, Paint Inside mode was used, and the brush strokes started outside the face.

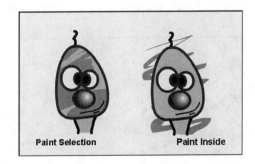

Nitty Gritty Stuff

Lock 'N Fill?

The Lock Fill option button is only relevant if you are applying a gradient fill (or bitmap fill) to a brush stroke. Gradient fills are examined in Chapter 5, "Have Your Fill." But briefly, they are fills that change color—for example from black to white, over the space of an object. When you activate the Lock Fill option, gradient fills are applied as if the fill was assigned to the entire stage, and the brush is simply "uncovering" a gradient fill on the underling stage. Without the Lock Fill option, gradients are stretched out to cover the length of the brush stroke, not the entire stage.

Erasing Objects

The Eraser tool is much more than a way to clean up junk you don't want. It comes with a complex set of options similar to those you get with the Brush tool. You can define eraser size and shape. And you can set the eraser to work on just fills, just lines, inside an object, or only inside a selected object.

Press **E** to select the Eraser tool, or click the tool in the **Drawing Toolbar**. The Eraser Shape option, shown in Figure 4.8, lets you choose from five sizes of round erasers, and five sizes of square erasers.

Figure 4.8

The eraser comes in two shapes and five sizes.

Easy Erase

If what you are trying to do is *delete* all or part of an object, the easiest way to do that is often to select the object by drawing a marquee around it with the **Select** (or **Lasso**) tool, and then just press the delete key. Save the Erase tool for when you want to fine-tune your erasing.

Figure 4.9

One click with the Faucet and the tail is gone.

Undoing the Eraser

Keep the Undo tool handy when you use the Faucet—sometimes you end up erasing more than you expected.

Cleaning Up with Erase

You can use the Eraser tool to make really tiny corrections in an existing drawing. When you zoom in to 800% and select the smallest eraser size, you can edit individual pixels—the tiniest element of a drawing.

Or, you can use the Eraser tool to cut objects in half—just as you would if you drew a line through them.

Turn On the Faucet

The Faucet option in the Eraser toolbar changes the way the eraser works. With the Faucet option selected, you can quickly erase any object (line or fill) that you click on. In Figure 4.9, we're about to delete an entire line.

Erase—It's a DRAW Tool

The Eraser Mode option works like the Brush Mode option. It changes the way the eraser reacts with a drawing.

Erase Fills erases *only* object fills, leaving lines untouched. Erase Lines whites out what you move the eraser over but does not erase fills.

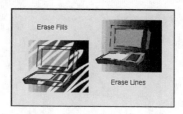

Figure 4.10
One eraser mode eats only lines; the other one eats only fills.

The Erase Selected Fills option works like this: First, use the Select tool to choose a fill; then, use the Eraser (with the Erase Selected Fills option) to erase *only* within the selected fill.

The Erase Inside option turns your eraser into a tool that erases *only within the object that you start erasing*. Figure 4.11 shows both erasing selected fills, and erasing "inside" an object.

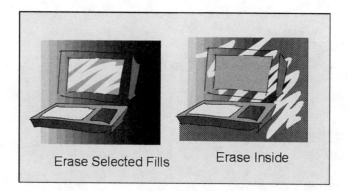

Figure 4.11
The erasing in the drawing on the left was done by first selecting the monitor screen. In the drawing on the right, the background was selected and erased

The Least You Need to Know

➤ Brush sizes and shapes can range from tiny to huge—if the largest size is too small, try zooming out to enlarge a brush size.

➤ Brush shapes are used to create lines of varying thickness.

➤ The Eraser tool replaces objects with white. Use the Faucet option to delete entire objects at once.

➤ Both the Brush and Eraser tools have options that allow you to delete just lines, just fills, or just parts of selected objects.

GLUG
GLUG
GLUG

Chapter 5

Have Your Fill

In This Chapter

➤ Defining fill colors for shapes

➤ Mixing up gradient fills for effect

➤ Changing your color palette text

➤ Managing the Paint Bucket to change fills

➤ Picking up and dropping off fills with the Dropper

➤ Changing outlines with the Ink Bottle

Flash gives you many options for controlling fills and outlines. You can keep life simple, and use the default color palette, or you can mix up your own colors and gradient fills for a little excitement.

Putting Colors to Work

The Fill Color Option icon in the Toolbox defines what color will be assigned to objects that you draw. When you click the Fill Color icon, you can choose colors from the color palette.

The default color set in Flash consists of 216 browser-safe colors. This is a handy color set because these colors are interpreted accurately by Web browsers.

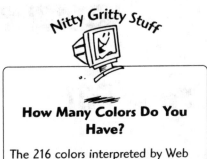

How Many Colors Do You Have?

The 216 colors interpreted by Web browsers are in addition to 40 colors set aside for operating systems. If you are creating a Flash movie for an environment where you know viewers will have access to a full 24-bit color monitor, you can use 16.7 million different colors in your movie.

Sometimes you want to increase or decrease the number of colors in your color palette. For example, if you are working on a project with an assigned color scheme that uses only eight colors, you can create a custom color palette with just those eight colors to make choosing your color fills quicker and easier.

Choosing and Changing Solid Fill Colors

When you click on the Fill Color icon, you open the flyout default color palette. The palette displays the current selected color in the upper left corner. You can select a color from the palette. Or, you can move your cursor anywhere in the Flash window or on your desktop (the cursor becomes an eyedropper), and click to assign the color in the Flash window to select a color. Selected colors are assigned to the Fill color icon.

If you want to change the color palette, or select colors not in the existing palette, choose **Window**, **Panels**, **Mixer** to open the Mixer panel, shown in Figure 5.1.

Figure 5.1

The Mixer panel allows you to choose from a wide array of colors.

To add a new color to your palette, click in the Color Bar, and choose **Add to Swatch** from the flyout menu, as shown in Figure 5.2.

The Figure 5.2

You can add new colors to your palettes with the Color Mixer.

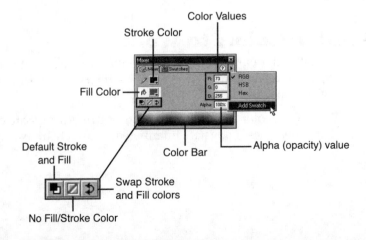

To select a color not in your palette, either click the color in the color space, or define a color by entering values in the **R**, **G**, and **B** areas. The new color will display in the Fill color area of the Mixer panel.

After you select a color, click the options flyout and click **Add Swatch** to add the color in the Selected Color display swatch to your palette.

Color by Number

The R, G, and B boxes in the Mixer panel allow you to assign Red, Green, or Blue values. This RGB system is a standard way of assigning colors.

The options flyout in the Mixer palette (shown in Figure 5.2) allows you to select alternate standardized methods for defining colors. The HSB system allows you to define hue, saturation, and brightness for a color, and the Hex system—often used by professional Web designers—is like the RGB system, but uses two-digit codes to identify colors.

Orchestrating Your Colors

Several handy options for managing your color palette appear when you open the Swatches panel (choose **Window**, **Panels**, **Swatches**).

The Save Colors option, shown in Figure 5.3, saves your current color palette as a file, so you can reuse it. The Save as Default option saves your current color palette as a new default color set for Flash. And the 216 Colors option loads the Web-safe, 216-color palette. Figure 5.3 shows this handy pop-up menu.

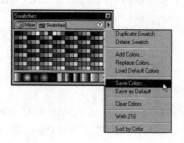

Figure 5.3

Handy options for managing color palettes include Save—which saves color palettes as reusable named files.

Nitty Gritty Stuff

Opacity Versus Transparency

Fills can have various degrees of opacity or transparency. A fully (100%) opaque fill would be completely solid, while a 0% Alpha fill is completely transparent.

How Transparent Can You Get?

The Alpha slider (to see it, click the down arrow next to the **Alpha** box in the Mixer panel) defines the degree of opacity in a fill. If you set the slider to 100%, your fill will be completely solid. Lower settings allow a fill to be transparent.

Because moving one shape over another (in the same layer) *cuts into* the second shape, you must first define a shape as a group (even if it's only one object) to take advantage of transparency. If you change a transparent object into a group, you can move it on top of other groups, to produce an effect like the one shown in Figure 5.4.

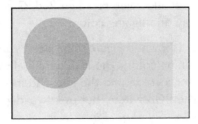

Figure 5.4

Moving a transparent-fill group over another group creates a "new look" in the overlapping areas of the groups.

Backstage Pass

Layering with Transparent Fills

While transparent objects must be grouped to stack on top of each other in a single layer, you can stack transparent layers on top of each other without grouping them if you place them in separate layers. Layers are covered in Chapter 8, "Working with Layers."

Blending Colors with Gradient Fills

Gradient fills are color fills that merge from one color to another. Gradients can be either Linear (progressing from one side to another) or Radial (starting in the center and progressing outward), see Figure 5.5.

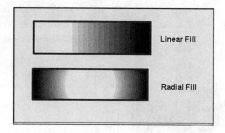

Figure 5.5

Linear and radial fills can add some depth and interest to your objects in Flash.

The Fill Color palette in the Toolbox comes with several predefined gradients. You can assign them to the Fill option just by clicking them.

To define a custom gradient fill, choose **Window**, **Panels**, **Fill** to view the Fill panel. The Fill panel and its key components are illustrated in Figure 5.6.

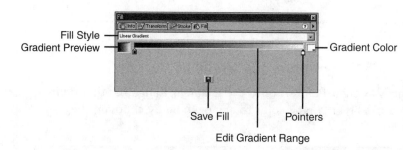

Figure 5.6

The colored bar above the Gradient Type pop-up menu is the Gradient Definition bar that shows you the various "steps" in the gradient you've chosen.

From the Fill Style drop-down list, choose either **Linear Gradient** or **Radial Gradient**. Underneath the Fill Style list is the Edit Gradient Range area, and underneath that wide strip are at least two pointers. These pointers can be moved, added, or removed to change the way colors merge into each other.

Move pointers by clicking them and dragging right or left. Remove pointers by dragging them down, away from the Gradient range area. Add pointers by clicking underneath the Gradient Range strip.

To change a color in a pointer:

1. Click the pointer.
2. Click the **Gradient Color** icon to open the color palette.
3. Select a color for the pointer. If you have the mixer panel open you can also pick colors from the color selector if you first click on one of the pointers.

After you define a gradient fill, click the **Save** button to add your fill to the swatches on the color palette. After you do that, your gradient fill will be available from the Fill Color options palette in the Toolbox, as shown in Figure 5.7.

Figure 5.7

After you define a gradient fill and click the Save button in the Fills panel, your gradient is assigned to the Fills option palette.

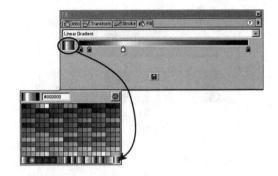

Backstage Pass

Many Colors in a Gradient

You can drag as many as eight Pointers onto the Gradient Range bar that defines a gradient. And you can assign a new color to any of them by choosing the Pointer.

Gradients can be a lot of fun, and can contribute to effects in drawings. In Figure 5.8, the gradient contributes to the message.

Figure 5.8

The gradient is the message: Using a dark-to-light color gradient as the graph area fill enhances the "going up" message of the graphic.

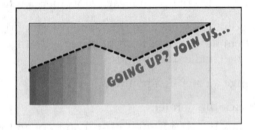

Get Out the Paint Bucket

You can *change* the existing fill of a shape using the Paint Bucket tool. The Fill Color option defines the color to be applied by the Paint Bucket. The Gap Size option lets you tell Flash how much to "stretch" when filling in drawings that aren't completely filled in (see Figure 5.9).

News Flash

Paying a Price for Gradients

Conventional wisdom *has been* to avoid gradients in Web graphics. Gradients don't tend to stand up well in traditional bitmap-based Web graphics because of the limited color palette, and the limits of those file formats in preserving colors. With Flash, however, you can maintain smooth, attractive colors in your gradient fills. The price is that each gradient color adds to your file size, and adds to the time it takes for a Flash movie to download into a browser.

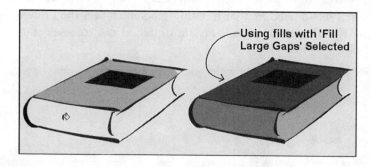

Using fills with 'Fill Large Gaps' Selected

Figure 5.9

The Paint Bucket can be used to fill in a shape (like the bottom of the book) that is not a completely filled in drawing.

Filling with the Paint Bucket

After you select a fill color (or gradient) from the Fill Color option in the Paint Bucket toolbox, use the Gap Size option to define how Flash will apply fills to areas.

Figure 5.10 shows the different options in the Gap Size option. If you select Don't Close Gaps, the Paint Bucket will apply fills only to shapes that are completely enclosed by lines. If you select Close Large Gaps, shapes that are not completely enclosed will have fills applied. The other settings fall in between.

Figure 5.10

Gap fill options for the Paint Bucket. I usually choose Close Large Gaps to help fill in shapes that are not completely closed.

Nitty Gritty Stuff

More Paintbrush Options

The Transform Fill option in the Toolbox is used with the Paint Bucket tool to apply a Flash vector–based fill to an imported bitmap fill. For more info on bitmaps see "Importing Bitmaps" in Chapter 20, "Getting Outside Help: Importing Objects."

The Lock Fill option affects the way gradient fills are applied to an object by the Paint Bucket. When you activate the Lock Fill option, gradient fills are applied as if the fill was assigned to the entire stage. With Lock Fill on, the object to which you are assigning a fill acts like a window that reveals a gradient fill on the underlying stage. *Without* the Lock Fill option, gradients are stretched out to cover the length of the *object*, not the entire stage.

Backstage Pass

Centering Gradient Fills

When you use the Paint Bucket to apply radial gradient fills, you can define where the "center" of your gradient fill will appear in a shape by where you click when you assign the fill. Try clicking with the Paint Bucket in different parts of a shape with a radial gradient fill to experiment with this effect. This doesn't work if you have Lock Fill turned on (see the previous "Nitty Gritty" note).

Reshaping Fills

When you create a fill, it is actually a distinct object. Of course, you can change its color (or gradient), but you can also reshape it. Do that by selecting the **Arrow** tool and moving your cursor over a fill until the curve-point or arrow-point cursors display. Use those cursors to click and drag on the edge of a fill to reshape it, as shown in Figure 5.11.

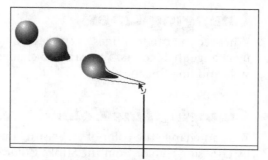

Figure 5.11

Fills can be resized and reshaped to fit more precisely with your objects.

Reshaping a fill with the curve-point cursor.

Borrowing Colors

The Dropper tool allows you to grab a color from one fill and "drop" it into another fill.

To "fill" the Dropper, select the **Dropper** tool from the toolbar (press **I**, as in I (eye) Dropper) Point the **Dropper** at a fill and click.

As soon as you click a fill with the Dropper tool, the cursor changes to a Paint Bucket tool cursor, along with a tiny lock indicating that the fill color is locked in until you click a shape.

Figure 5.12 shows a fill being transferred in the Dropper into another shape.

Backstage Pass

Fill 'er Up—Quick

You need not use the paint bucket to change fills. Here's a shortcut: Simply select a fill area on the stage, then click on the Fill Color button in the Toolbox and select a color.

Figure 5.12

"Dropping" a fill from one shape into another is easier than creating the fill for each object from scratch.

The Dropper cursor changes to a Paint Bucket cursor when "loaded" with a fill.

67

Bailing Out on the Dropper

If you have loaded the dropper with a color, and then decide you *don't* want to drop that color into another fill, you can bail out by choosing the Arrow tool. This undoes the dropper process.

Changing Lines

Whether you call 'em lines or strokes, you can easily change their colors. You can also change line style and line thickness.

Changing Line Color

You can change the color of an existing line (stroke) by choosing a color from the Stroke Color palette. Access that color palette by clicking the **Stroke Color** option icon in the Toolbox.

With a new line color loaded into the Stroke Color icon, press **S** to select the Ink Bottle tool. Then click a line with the Ink Bottle to apply the new color, as shown in Figure 5.13.

Figure 5.13

You can change line color with the Ink Bottle.

Grouped Objects Don't Respond to the Ink Bottle

You cannot use the Ink Bottle on grouped objects. If you need to change the outline of a grouped object, ungroup it first. The same goes for fills.

You can also change the outline color by selecting the outline and clicking on the Stroke Color option and selecting a color. The Ink Bottle is a quick way of changing a *bunch of outlines* to a specific color.

Some shapes don't have outlines, but you can still use the Ink Bottle tool on them. Clicking a shape without an outline applies the attributes selected in the Ink Bottle options to a shape—in effect creating an outline for that shape.

Changing Line Height and Style

To change the height or style of existing lines, first activate the Stroke panel by choosing **Window, Panels, Stroke**.

From the Stroke panel, use the **Stroke Style** drop-down menu to choose a stroke type. Use the **Stroke Height** box to define the thickness of the line. You can choose colors from the **Stroke color** swatch in the Stroke panel if you want (you can also do this from the **Stroke Color options** icon in the Toolbox).

The stroke style and height you define in the Stroke panel will be applied to the attributes of the Ink Bottle. So after you define Stroke attributes, use the Ink Bottle to apply them to any line, as shown in Figure 5.14.

Figure 5.14

The Stroke attributes (gray dashed line) defined in the Stroke panel are applied with the Ink Bottle to existing lines.

The Least You Need to Know

➤ Fills can be solid colors or gradients that combine up to eight colors that blend into each other.

➤ Choose fill colors from the Fill Color flyout palette in the Toolbox.

➤ Choose Linear Gradient or Radial Gradient from the Fill Style drop-down menu in the Fill panel to define new gradient fills.

➤ The default 216-color, Web-safe palette displays colors that are interpreted reliably by Web browsers. Stick with them and you won't go wrong.

➤ The Paint Bucket tool allows you to apply new fills to existing shapes.

➤ The Dropper tool grabs a color from one fill and applies it to another fill.

➤ The Ink Bottle tool changes the color, thickness, and style of existing lines depending on attributes you define in the Stroke panel.

SNIP

Chapter 6

Snip, Snap, Stick

In This Chapter

➤ Selecting objects

➤ Reshaping drawings

➤ Grouping objects

➤ Moving drawings in front of and behind each other

➤ Fine tuning drawings and curves with the Subselect tool

Imagine yourself directing a movie with thousands of actors. Okay, we're not talking about an intimate romantic comedy here—more like "Earth Versus Mars" or something. But you're in the director's chair and you want to move *one* actor, or a group of actors, to another location. Just yelling "Hey you...move right" might send hundreds of extras off a cliff!

I pose this draconian scenario to emphasize how useful it is to be able to select objects and groups of objects in Flash. As you work with complex movies involving techniques we have yet to explore, you'll greatly appreciate the ability to select and control objects on your stage.

Movin' and Shakin'

Backstage Pass

Type "V" for Arrow?

To select the Arrow tool, press **V** on your keyboard. A, which used to activate the Arrow key in Flash 4, now activates the Subselect tool, which we'll explore later in this chapter.

There are two tools that are used to select objects on the stage—the Arrow tool and the Lasso tool. The Lasso tool is handy for roping in disparate objects, but the Arrow tool is where most of the serious business of selecting and changing objects goes down.

When you choose the Select tool, the toolbox displays options that are used to reshape, resize, and rotate selected objects. They're identified in Figure 6.1. Cut this out, paste it on your monitor, and refer to it later. Actually, a sticky note on this page might be a better idea—that way you can read this page again later!

Figure 6.1

The Arrow tool is used to select and change an object.

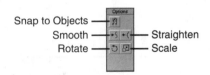

The option Snap to Objects tool makes objects on the stage take on a "magnetic" quality (view it by choosing **View, Snap**) to help move objects next to each other. The Smooth and Straighten tools convert zigzags to curves and vice versa.

The Rotate and Scale options let you change the size, shape and rotation angle of objects.

Three Faces of the Arrow Tool

The Arrow tool (press **V** on the keyboard to activate it) works three ways. It can be used to select an object, to change an object curve, or to change an object shape.

Backstage Pass

Where Is That Darn Curved Line Selection Cursor?

The curved line cursor tends to appear when you move your cursor over the middle of a line.

Which is which? As you hover your Select cursor over an object, you can change the appearance of the cursor by moving it ever so slightly across the edge of a shape or line. You'll see the cursor switch between a box and a curved line.

When the curved line Selection tool icon is visible, you can click and drag on a line to change the curve (as shown in Figure 6.2).

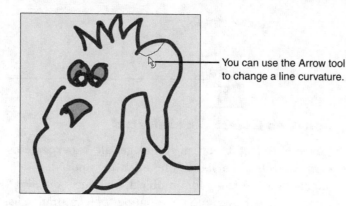

Figure 6.2

Selecting a line to change the curve.

You can use the Arrow tool to change a line curvature.

When you move the Arrow tool cursor toward the end of a line, it displays as an inverted L. You can click and drag with this icon to change the size and direction of a line, as shown in Figure 6.3.

Figure 6.3

Or...use the Arrow tool to change a line length.

Finally, you can select an object *just to select it* by clicking on the object. When you do, the object appears grayed out, as shown in Figure 6.4.

Selected Object

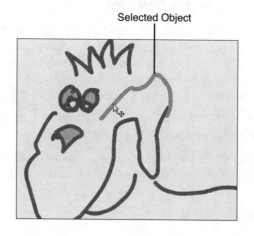

Figure 6.4

You can use the Arrow key to move selected objects. You can tell the Arrow key is in "move mode" by the four-sided arrow cursor.

Backstage Pass

Only *One Object* Gets Selected

When you click on an object to select it, you might not get all you expected. Flash often generates *many* objects when you create a drawing. Individual line segments are distinct objects, as is the filling for an object. To select adjoining objects, try double-clicking. To select even more contiguous objects, triple click. Want to select with a bit more precision? Read the next section.

Backstage Pass

Quick Ways to Select Stuff

If you want to select everything in your movie, choose **Edit**, **Select All**. The keyboard shortcut is (Cmd-A) [Ctrl+A]. You can deselect (unselect) everything by choosing **Edit**, **Deselect All**, or by pressing (Cmd-Shift-A) [Ctrl+Shift+A].

Selecting Many Objects

Often you'll want to select more than one object to cut, copy, paste, resize, or move, especially now that you realize just how many objects can exist in a single drawing!

To select additional objects, hold down the Shift key while you point and click at objects in a drawing.

Selecting Rectangular Areas and Lassoing Objects

If you are going to be selecting a bunch of objects, you'll get tired of Shift-clicking over and over. An easier way to select a bunch of objects is to use the Arrow tool to draw a rectangle (sometimes called a selection marquee) around the objects, as shown in Figure 6.5.

To select an irregularly shaped set of objects, use the Lasso tool. Press **L** on the keyboard or just click the Lasso icon in the toolbox to select the Lasso tool.

Click and draw with the Lasso tool as you would if you were drawing an object. Use the Lasso tool to outline a section of the Stage to include all objects within the Lasso in your selection.

Figure 6.6 shows the Lasso tool being used to select several objects.

Figure 6.5

Drawing a selection marquee is as simple as drawing a box around your object or group of objects.

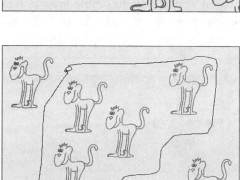

Figure 6.6

Using the Lasso tool to round up some monkeys.

The Lasso tool has an option that allows you to toggle Polygon mode on or off. Turning on Polygon mode changes the way the Lasso tool works. With Polygon mode on, you can't simply draw outlines of a selection area; you have to click where you want segments to end. End the process by double-clicking to create an enclosed polygon of selected objects.

The other options in the Lasso tool allow you to attempt to select sections of graphics that have been converted from bitmap graphic files—pictures that you import into Flash.

If you want to select all the objects on the Stage, choose **Edit, Select All** from the menu. To deselect everything on the Stage, choose **Edit, Deselect All**.

Backstage Pass

Lassoing Bunches of Objects

You can create complex selections by first selecting one group of objects with the Lasso tool, and then selecting another group with either the Select or Lasso tool *while holding down the Shift key.*

Backstage Pass

Bitmaps Come Later

The magic wand options don't really fit that well with the Lasso tool—they're used for working with images created by programs that use bitmapped pixels instead of Flash's smooth and efficient vector logic to define graphic files. Advanced Flash designers will one-day need to interact with the bitmap world, and when and if you do, refer to the discussion of bitmaps in Chapter 20, "Getting Outside Help: Importing Objects."

News Flash

Watch What You Selected (and Did Not Select)

Because most drawings are composed of many objects, it's easy to *think* you selected a drawing, when actually you only selected *some* of the objects in a drawing. For example, if you click on a shape *fill*, you *only select the fill*, not the outline object(s) if there are any. To play it safe, use the Select (or Lasso) tool to draw a nice wide selection marquee around your object. *Only objects that are completely enclosed* in a selection marquee get selected.

When an object doesn't get completely surrounded by the Lasso, unselected areas that are "left out" of the selection area end up as a new object.

Straightening and Curving Selections

The Smooth and Straighten options in the Arrow tool can be used to convert drawings from jagged to smooth, or vice versa.

To smooth a drawing, select all the desired objects in the drawing, select the Arrow tool, and click the Smooth icon in the Options area of the toolbox. To turn rounded corners into angled lines, click the Straighten icon in the Toolbox. To increase the amount of smoothing or straightening, click the Smooth or Straighten icons more than once.

Figure 6.7 shows the effect of smoothing and straightening lines in selected objects.

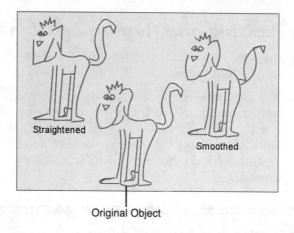

Straightened

Smoothed

Original Object

Figure 6.7

Selected objects can be smoothed or straightened.

Copying, Cutting, and Moving Objects

Selected objects can be easily cut, copied, or moved. A selected object (or bunch of selected objects) can be moved by clicking and dragging. With either the Select or Lasso tools active, a selected bunch of objects displays a four-pointed arrow when you hover over the center of the selection. Click and drag *using that four-pointed arrow* to move objects, as shown in Figure 6.8.

Backstage Pass

Moving to Spots

If you hold down the Shift key as you drag on selected objects, you'll turn on an invisible "magnetic" line that helps move the object in a straight line horizontally, vertically, or diagonally (at a 45° angle).

New location of selected object

Original location of selected object

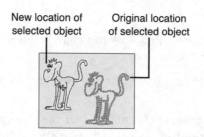

Figure 6.8

Moving a bunch of objects at once—as you move the objects, a new version of the objects appears along with the original until you release the mouse button.

Quick Dups

To create a quick duplicate of selected objects, press (Cmd-D) [Ctrl+D] (for "D"uplicate—get it?). Or, hold down the Control key as you click and drag on a selected object to leave the original in place and create a duplicate.

You can cut or copy a selected bunch of objects to the clipboard by choosing **Edit, Cut** or **Edit, Copy**. You can paste objects from the Clipboard by choosing **Edit, Paste**.

Resizing and Reshaping Objects

The Scale option in the Arrow toolbar allows you to re-size or reshape objects.

With objects selected, click the Scale option to display eight sizing squares on the corners and sides of the selected object(s). Click and drag on side, top, or bottom handles to reshape the object(s), or click and drag on the corner handles to resize the object, as shown in Figure 6.9.

Figure 6.9

Clicking and dragging on corner sizing squares maintains the original shape of objects while they are being resized.

Rotating Objects

Clicking the Rotate option in the Arrow toolbar activates eight rotation circles on the corners and sides of the selected object(s).

The corner rotation circles let you click and drag to rotate objects, as shown in Figure 6.10.

Clicking and dragging on the *side* rotation circles moves *only* the side you select. Use this feature to create some fun distortions of your drawing, as shown in Figure 6.11.

Rotate handle

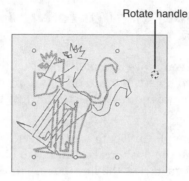

Figure 6.10

Rotating selected objects creates a funky new look for your object.

Figure 6.11

Clicking and dragging on side Rotation circles moves only the selected side of objects. The effect is like that of a lever with the "fulcrum," or turning point, being the rotation handle opposite from the selected one.

Combining Objects into Groups

Almost every drawing is made up of more than one object—even drawing a simple curve can produce many objects. It's often useful to combine objects so that you can move and edit them all at once.

Grouping objects temporarily changes them into a single object that can be moved or modified. And, if you later want to work on just one object in a group, you can ungroup the objects.

To group a set of objects, use the Arrow or Lasso tool to select the objects, and then choose **Modify, Group**.

To ungroup, click with the Arrow tool to select a grouped object, and choose **Modify, Ungroup**.

You cannot modify the line attribute or fill attribute of a group.

News Flash

Grouping Prevents Accidents

Grouping is great in that it prevents you from moving or changing part of a drawing accidentally. Think of Grouping as a way of protecting a drawing! Grouped objects can always be ungrouped if you want to touch up a single object.

Grouping Groups

Can you group a bunch of grouped objects? Sure—just use the Arrange or Lasso tool to select more than one grouped object, and choose **Modify, Group**.

Moving Groups to the Front or Back

When you move a *grouped* object on top of another grouped object, the two objects don't "cut each other up" the way normal objects do when they intersect in Flash.

For example, in Figure 6.12, the vertical line drawn through the oval breaks it into two objects that can be moved apart. But the line drawn "through" the grouped objects that form the monkey does not break the monkey in half.

Figure 6.12

Because the monkey is a grouped object, the line does not cut it in half.

When two grouped objects intersect, one sits on top of the other. You can change the stacking order for grouped objects by selecting a grouped object with the Arrow tool.

Grouping Versus Layers

For serious piling up layers of objects, you'll want to use different layers for different objects. This is covered in Chapter 8, "Working with Layers." But if you just want to move one grouped object behind another, you can use the Arrange feature.

With the grouped object selected, choose **Modify, Arrange**. You can then choose from:

➤ **Bring to Front**—Move the selected grouped object in front of all other grouped objects on the Stage.

➤ **Bring Forward**—Move the selected grouped object in front of the grouped objects that it intersects with.

➤ **Send Backwards**—Move the selected grouped object behind the grouped objects that it intersects with.

➤ **Send to Back**—Move the selected grouped object behind *all* other grouped objects on the Stage.

Figure 6.13 shows grouped objects moved in front of and behind each other.

Figure 6.13

The incarcerated monkey on the left has been moved "behind" the bars, while the free monkey on the right has been moved in front of the bars.

Locking Grouped Objects

Locking grouped objects is like sticking them in a safe-deposit box at the bank. You can't move 'em, you can't change 'em, but on the other hand you can't mess them up. To lock a grouped object, select it and choose **Modify, Arrange, Lock**.

Microediting with the Subselect Tool

A new feature in Flash 5 is the Subselect tool. With it, you can move and control curve points (nodes).

Choose the Subselect tool from the Toolbox with your mouse, or press the letter A on your keyboard. As you select objects with the Subselect tool, nodal points appear, as shown in Figure 6.14.

News Flash

You Can't Select Locked Groups

After you lock a grouped object, not only can you not edit or move it, you can't even select it. The only way to unlock an object is to choose **Modify, Arrange, Unlock All**.

Backstage Pass

How Are Curves Defined?

As a vector-based drawing program, Flash defines curves by nodal points and by the curvature of lines that connect them. Think of creating a drawing using a "connect the dots" puzzle, and you have the basic logic of Flash.

Figure 6.14

The subselect tool displays dozens of small nodal points in the ears and head of the rabbit.

Moving Nodes

Once you select an object with the Subselect tool, you can move individual curve nodes. As you move your Subselect cursor next to a curve node, the cursor changes to a hollow square. Click and drag on the curve node to edit the curve, as shown in Figure 6.15.

News Flash

First Ungroup

To use the Subselect tool, first un-group the object you want to edit.

Figure 6.15

Moving a single node on a curve.

82

Editing Curves with Control Points

For the ultimate in curve control, you can adjust the two control points that come with every curve. To edit curve control points, it helps to magnify your drawing quite a bit.

With a node selected (using the Subselect tool), click and drag on either of the control points associated with that curve.

You can change the curvature of a line by extending control points (dragging them away from the curve nodal point), or shortening them. Shortening the control point lines makes a curve tighter, while stretching them makes a curve wider, as shown in Figure 6.16.

Backstage Pass

Maxing Out on Magnification

Even though the View drop-down menu in the Status Bar maxes out at 400%, you can manually enter higher numbers up to 2000% to *really* zoom in on a drawing.

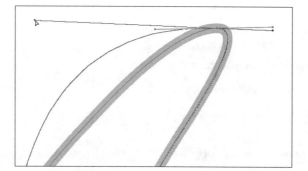

Figure 6.16

Lengthening control point lines to make a curve wider.

You can also adjust curves by dragging control points clockwise or counterclockwise. Figure 6.17 shows a curve being altered by rotating the right control point in a clockwise direction.

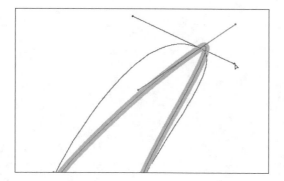

Figure 6.17

In this drawing, rotating the right curve control point clockwise is widening the curve. Since the control point lines are of different lengths (the right side is shorter), the changes to the curve are happening mainly on the left side.

83

Backstage Pass

Microtuning—It's Not for Everyone

Tweaking curve control points is reserved for very fine tuning of drawings. Many of us use it rarely, if at all. But when you need ultimate control over curves, the Subselect tool allows you to adjust them with control points.

The Least You Need to Know

➤ Before you can change an object, use the Arrow or Lasso tool to select it.

➤ The Arrow tool displays as either a curve, a square or a four-sided arrow. The curve icon changes line curves, the square changes line length and direction, and the four-sided arrow allows you to move objects.

➤ Objects can be grouped for easy editing.

➤ The Subselect tool displays tiny curve nodes in drawings that can be moved or edited.

Part 3
Setting the Stage

Life is a whole lot easier if everything is set up just right. Flash is the same way. In the following chapters, you'll learn to work with 3-D layers to organize your movie.

You'll also learn to integrate text into your movie, and pick up a few tricks to make your text wild, fun, and protected against the unpredictable ways that browsers handle text.

Chapter 7

Stage Design

In This Chapter

➤ Sizing objects with rulers

➤ Changing how grids and guides are displayed

➤ Snapping objects into place

➤ Defining stage size

➤ Changing movie background color

The *Stage* is the white part of the drawing area—and only the objects that you place on the Stage appear in movies. You can control how the Stage works by turning on features like the ruler or grid lines that help you size and locate objects.

The Stage is also a design element. By changing the size and background color of a Stage, you change how your movie appears in the Flash viewer, or in a Web browser.

What Are Stage Elements?

When you need to design complex sets of shapes, you will want to customize the Stage. Customizing the Stage can help you line up objects, change the background of a movie frame, and define object sizes.

Stage elements that help you design and locate objects include

➤ Rulers

➤ Grid lines to help you line up and size objects

➤ Customizable Guide lines to help you place objects

➤ The Snap feature that activates grid lines

Nitty Gritty Stuff

The Stage and the Timeline

The Flash environment kind of functions in three dimensions: The *Timeline* at the top of the Flash window controls the sequential display of your movie frames. The Timeline is covered in Part 6 of this book, "Animating with Flash Movies." Just about everything else in Flash takes place on the Stage—the area where you actually design the frames in your movie.

Using Rulers

A quick easy way to size objects on the Stage is to display a ruler. No, not one you pull out of your desk drawer, the one that comes built in with Flash. To do this, choose **View**, **Rulers** from the menu. Horizontal and vertical rulers appear on the top and left side of the Stage.

When you select an object on the Stage, small ticks appear in the rulers, indicating the dimensions of the object. For example, the monkey in Figure 7.1 is about 100 pixels high.

Figure 7.1

Need a 100 pixel-high rabbit? Set ruler units to pixels and quickly space the fella' using the ruler.

Units of Measurement

In Figure 7.1, the units of measurement on the ruler are set to *pixels*—a useful way to measure graphics intended for Web and monitor display, where images are composed of pixels (dots).

You can change the unit of measurement for your Stage by choosing **Modify**, **Movie**, and selecting a unit of measurement from the Ruler Units pop-up menu. Then, click **OK** to change the ruler display. Ruler Unit options include inches, points, centimeters, and millimeters.

Creating Custom Guides

You can mark ruler lines on the Stage by creating customized guides. These guides can then be used to locate or align objects on the Stage.

For example, if you wanted to line up one object vertically with another object, you could define a horizontal guide, and align both objects with that guide.

To create a guide, you must first have rulers displayed. Click and drag on a ruler, pulling the ruler onto the Stage. As you do, you create a guide, as shown in Figure 7.2.

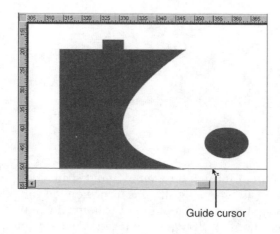

Guide cursor

Figure 7.2

As you drag a guide onto the Stage, the guide cursor appears. You can remove guides by clicking on them and dragging them back into the horizontal or vertical ruler.

To activate the guides you place on the Stage, choose **View, Guides** from the menu, and make sure Snap to Guides is selected.

With Snap to Guides turned on, guide lines work like magnets, attracting objects that are dragged near them. You can define the "power" of these magnets in the Guides dialog box by choosing **View, Guides, Edit Guides** to display the dialog box. The Snap Accuracy drop-down list allows you to choose from three levels of pull-toward guide lines: Must Be Close (least pull), Normal, and Can Be Distant (most pull).

Grids and Snaps

Another easy way to quickly size and locate objects on the Stage is to use grids. *Grids* are horizontal and vertical lines that display on the Stage. As with guide lines, grids do not show up when visitors watch your movie.

When you display grids and turn on snap, you can easily move and size objects to sizes and locations marked by grids.

Displaying Grids

To turn on grid display, choose **View, Grid**, and select **Show Grid**. You can change the color of the grid display by choosing **View, Grid, Edit Grid** from the menu. The Color pop-up palette allows you to change the color of a grid. The Show Grid and Snap to Grid check boxes display and activate grids respectively. The horizontal and vertical grid boxes allow you to enter any distance as spacing between gridlines.

Experiment with the Snap Accuracy drop-down menu in the Grid dialog box. It provides four different sensitivity settings that determine how powerful a "pull" will be exerted on objects as you move them towards a grid. Figure 7.3 shows the Grid dialog box.

Figure 7.3

Setting the Snap Accuracy to "Must Be Close" is useful when you want to align some objects close to, but not right on, a snap line.

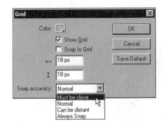

Turning on Snap

Grids don't do a heck of a lot without turning on *snap*. Without snap, grids just display, but with snap, their function as "magnetic" lines is turned on. As you pull an object toward a grid line with snap turned on, your object will literally jump to the location of the nearest grid line. Choosing **View, Snap** toggles Snap on and off.

Best to Leave Grid Background Alone

The Grid dialog box allows you to define is the color of the grid lines by choosing a color from the Color palette. Choose this color based on what makes it easy for you to see grid lines on the stage as you design your presentation. The grid will not be visible when the movie is presented, so the grid lines will not appear and will not be part of the Stage background.

Snap On—Snap Off

The keyboard shortcut for turning on Snap to Grid is (Cmd-Shift-+) [Ctrl+Shift++]. The keyboard shortcut for turning on Snap to Guides is (Cmd-Shift-;) [Ctrl+Shift+;]. The keyboard shortcut for turning on Snap to Objects is (Cmd-Shift-/) [Ctrl+Shift+/].

Sometimes you will want to locate an object near another object (or a gridline or guideline), but not *right next to* the object. In that case, you'll want to turn *off* the relevant snap so you have the freedom to position your object *independent* of the "gravitational pull" of nearby objects, grid lines, or guide lines.

Aligning Objects to Snap or Guide Lines

You align objects with a grid or guide line by clicking and dragging them near the line, and letting the snap property do its magic. The power of the snap will depend on the Snap accuracy setting in the Grid dialog box. Choose **View, Grid, Edit** to open the Grid dialog box.

As you select an object with the arrow tool, if snap is on, a circle appears at the cursor point indicating the spot in the object that will snap to grid lines, as shown in Figure 7.4.

Figure 7.4

The monkey's nose has been selected as the snap spot and can be used to align the nose with any grid line.

Location, Location, Location?

When you animate objects, you essentially change their location from frame to frame. That's why the ability to easily and accurately place objects on the Stage using rulers and grids becomes essential when you move from designing objects to animating them.

Locking Guides and Grids

Both the Grid and Guides dialog boxes have a Locked check box. Selecting this check box locks the location of defined grids and guides, and prevents you from moving or deleting them.

Not Completely Locked...

You *can* delete grids and guides with the Lock check box selected if you click on the Clear All button in the Grid or Guides dialog box.

The Lock feature is especially helpful to prevent accidentally moving guides.

If later you need to move or edit grids or guides, just uncheck the Lock check box in the dialog box.

Aesthetics of Stage Design

Some Stage features are invisible after a movie is shown. Others affect how the movie will look. Movie background colors appear behind every frame when a movie is displayed.

Stage size also affects how a movie will be displayed. Stage size determines the overall size of a movie. If your movie is too big for the screen, you'll have problems. Like what? Well, think about that notice that appears on your TV when you watch a video at home. A warning appears telling you that the movie was cropped to fit your TV screen size. To avoid that kind of problem…read on.

Setting Stage Size

When you present your Flash movie in a Web browser, only those objects that are in the Stage (the white area) display. The objects outside the Stage—in the gray area—do not display in a movie.

Figure 7.5 shows a drawing where some of the objects are not included in the movie that will display in a browser.

Figure 7.5

Sorry! Only objects on the Stage get included in movies.

Backstage Pass

Storage Space

Because objects outside the Stage (in the gray area surrounding the Stage) do *not* display in movies, you can use this space to store some graphics objects you might want to use later in a frame. For serious storage of objects you want to reuse in many frames, check out the discussion of symbols and libraries in Part 4, "Hanging Out at the Recycling Center."

By defining the size of the Stage, you can control how a movie will display in the Flash viewer or in a Web browser. Normally, you will want the Stage to be big enough to display everything you draw, but not go beyond what the viewer's screen can show.

You can shrink the movie size to be just large enough to include everything on the stage by choosing **Modify**, **Movie**, and clicking the **Contents** button in the Movie dialog box. Clicking this button automatically shrinks the size of the Stage to include only enough space to accommodate the contents of the stage. The calculated size of the Stage will display in the Height and Width boxes in the Movie dialog box.

News Flash

Size Matters

If a Stage is too small to include all objects, the objects outside the Stage won't display in a movie. But if the Stage is larger than a browser window or monitor screen, viewers will miss part of the movie because objects will move "off the screen" unless a visitor uses his or her scroll bar to chase around after the action. Solution: Keep your movie size small enough to fit in a Web browser.

For a full exploration of how different sized movies interact with browsers, see the section "Embedding a Flash Movie in a Web Page," in Chapter 21 of this book.

Backstage Pass

Using Grouped Objects as Background Images

Using grouped objects as mini-layers to provide backgrounds is discussed in Chapter 6, "Snip, Snap, Stick."

Setting Background Color

Specific backgrounds for different objects can be defined by creating grouped objects behind other grouped objects. For instance, you can place a blue pond behind a boat by drawing the pond, and then moving a boat in front of it.

Layering groups can provide specific backgrounds for frames or objects, but you can also change the background color for an *entire movie*. To do that, choose **Modify**, **Movie** and click the **Background** pop-up menu. From the color palette, choose a color that will be the default background for all layers, and all frames in your movie.

Backstage Pass

No Gradients Here

Unfortunately, Flash doesn't allow gradients as background colors, so stick to a solid color from the palette. If you *really* want a gradient background, you can put a gradient object at the lowest layer in your movie. Layers are discussed in Chapter 8, "Working with Layers."

The Least You Need to Know

➤   You can turn on rulers, grids, and custom-defined guides in the View menu.

➤   Grids plus the Snap feature make it easy to position and size objects.

➤   Changing the size of your Stage determines how big your movie will appear in a browser window.

➤   Only objects that are on the Stage will appear in a movie.

➤   Changing the background color for a movie affects *all* frames and all levels of the movie.

Chapter 8

Working with Layers

In This Chapter

➤ Using layers to place objects in front of and behind each other

➤ Adding new layers

➤ Locking layers

➤ Displaying layers as outlines

➤ Hiding and showing layers

➤ Changing the order of layers

➤ Using layers as guides

➤ Creating mask layers that display parts of masked layers

Layers are transparent sheets that sit on top of each other, allowing you to stack objects on top of each other without worrying about messing them up, as can happen with intersecting objects in a single layer.

Layers make it easier to manage and edit a movie. For example, you might create a background layer that just has elements that stay behind everything else in the movie. On top of that you can create layers for different sets of objects to make it easy to edit those objects one at a time.

Finally, masked layers can be used to create a "peek hole" affect, where a see-through object can move to display different parts of underlying layers.

Beyond Drawing in One Dimension

In earlier chapters, you explored how intersecting drawings and shapes interfere with each other. For example, the monkey and tree in Figure 8.1 are both fairly complex drawings. Editing them will be a whole lot easier if each has its own layer.

Figure 8.1

By placing different objects on different layers, you eliminate the danger of dissecting shapes or lines when you move an object on top of another object.

In Figure 8.2, the same objects have their own layers, along with additional layers for background objects like the ground and the sky. This makes it easy to move objects around in relation to each other without damaging objects on other layers.

Backstage Pass

The Many Layers of Animation

Imagine a movie where a background stays in place, figures move around the screen, and text appears and moves across the screen. Organizing a movie like this is a whole lot easier if the background, text, and figures are all on their own separate layers. That way, each layer can be animated separately and later meshed with the rest of the movie.

In this movie, different layers can be edited individually.

Figure 8.2

Giving objects a layer of their own makes animating and editing these objects easier and quicker.

Getting to the Next Layer

Layers are most easily controlled and organized in the *Timeline*. You can use the Timeline to create layers, move layers in front of (or behind) each other, rename layers, change the properties of layers, and delete layers.

The other way to control layers is to use the menu. **Insert, Layer** inserts a new layer in your movie—right above the selected layer. The menu option for controlling layers is to choose **Modify, Layers**. This opens the Layer Properties dialog box for the layer you have selected. The options in the Layer Property box duplicate the features you control with icons in the Timeline. Since the icons are easier to access while you work, we'll focus on those in this section.

Nitty Gritty Stuff

Layers Versus Groups

In Chapter 6, "Snip, Snap, Stick," I discussed how groups can be used to keep objects from cutting each other up on a single layer. Groups are similar to layers, but layers are easier to organize and more efficient for large projects.

Adding (or Deleting) Layers

To add a layer, choose **Insert**, **Layer** from the menu. A new layer will display in the Timeline, on top of the stage. The new layer will appear at the top of existing layers, and will have the rather uncreative name of "Layer 2." Any additional layers will be named Layer 3, Layer 4, and so on.

You can change layer names by double-clicking on the current layer name and typing a new name, as shown in Figure 8.3.

Figure 8.3

Changing the layer name from the default to something that describes the object helps you keep track of your layers.

Backstage Pass

Adding Different Kinds of Layers

The + symbol at the bottom of the list of layers works in the same way as choosing **Insert**, **Layer** from the menu. The button next to it, the **Add Guide Layer** button, inserts a special kind of layer used in animation. Guide layers are discussed in Chapter 16, "Automating Animation."

Looking at Multiple Layers

After you have created more than one layer, you can switch layers by clicking on a layer in the Timeline.

At the top of the list of layers in the Timeline you'll find a set of icons that control whether, and how, a layer will be displayed, and whether you can edit a layer. Clicking on an icon at the top of the list of layers affects *all* layers, whereas clicking on that same icon in the row of a single layer affects only that layer.

The icons that control layer display are shown in Figure 8.4.

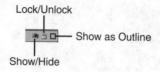

Lock/Unlock

Show as Outline

Show/Hide

Figure 8.4

Icons control how layers are displayed and whether you can edit them.

The Show/Hide icon either displays or hides a layer. This comes in real handy when you want to focus on editing a single layer, or you want to see how the objects on only certain layers look together.

The Lock/Unlock icon toggles between locking a layer to prevent it from being edited, and allowing editing. This is a safety feature that keeps you from ruining a layer by accident. Locked layers are safe from harm while you edit other layers.

News Flash

Careful! You Can Edit Multiple Layers at a Time...

If you don't lock a layer, you can edit objects on that layer even while you have a different layer selected. The way this works is that if you click on an object on a layer different than the selected layer, Flash automatically switches you to the layer with the selected object. This way you can edit across layers. Editing with several layers unlocked can be more convenient, but it can also be more confusing. When you start using layers, you may want to keep only one layer unlocked until you get comfortable with jumping back and forth between layers.

The Show as Outline icon displays the selected layer as an outline.

In Figure 8.5, the sun layer is hidden, the monkey layer is locked, the trees are displayed as outlines, and the ground layer is selected for editing.

To delete a layer, simply select it and click the Delete Layer icon, as shown in Figure 8.6.

You can also edit objects on layers that are not selected. It's harder to edit an object on a non-selected layer, but it can be done. When you click on an object—even if it's not on a selected layer—you can edit it.

Figure 8.5

You can tell which layers have display options chosen for them by looking to see what icons are showing at the right of the layer's name.

Figure 8.6

Sending a layer to the trash removes it from the Layers list and the Stage.

News Flash

Locking Doesn't Prevent Trashing

Locking a layer does *not* prevent you from deleting it by accident. Luckily you still have the **Edit**, **Undo** feature to save inadvertently destroyed layers. And, Flash *will not* allow you to delete the last layer in a movie.

As a general rule, you will want to do serious editing on a layer by hiding other layers and focusing on the objects on that single layer. On the other hand, if you want to arrange objects all at once in relation to each other, you'll want to do that with several layers displayed, and you'll want to move or edit objects on different layers at once.

Backstage Pass

Throwing Layers a Curve

Flash allows you to do *some* edits without changing the active layer. But editing across layers can produce unexpected results. If you click and drag on a filled object it will switch layers. If, on the other hand, you tweak a curve (click and drag) then the current active layer remains current and doesn't switch to the curve's layer.

Backstage Pass

The Benefit of Outline View

Viewing layers in Outline view makes it fast and easy to move a lot of objects around. Especially if computer memory is an issue, outline reduces memory demands on your system while you manipulate many layers at once.

You can also change the color that displays when you view a layer as an outline. Do this by selecting the layer and choosing **Modify**, **Layer**. Click the **Color** pop-up button in the Layer Properties dialog box to assign a color of your own choosing to the outline for the selected layer.

Movin' Layers Front and Back

Layers can be moved in front of or behind each other by changing their order in the layer list. Do that by clicking and dragging on a layer. For example, in Figure 8.7, the sun layer has been moved in front of the sky layer by dragging it in the Layers list and dropping it above the sky layer.

Figure 8.7

The sun has been moved behind the tree, but in front of the sky by changing the order of layers in the Timeline.

Assigning Properties to Many Layers

You can assign properties to groups of contiguous layers (layers next to each other) by using the Shift key as you click to select layers. Or, in Windows use Ctrl + click to select two or more layers that are not next to each other.

Editing Across Layers

Cutting and pasting between layers is pretty easy; first use the Arrow (or Lasso) tool to select an object or objects. Then choose **Edit**, **Copy** or **Edit**, **Cut** to move the object into the Clipboard.

With an object (or objects) in the Clipboard, click in the Timeline to select a layer, and choose **Edit**, **Paste** to place that object in a new layer.

Special Types of Layers

In addition to layers that display objects in your movie, Flash can generate two other types of layers: Guide layers and Mask layers.

Guide layers are layers that don't display in your movie. They define a path for generating animation.

Mask layers allow you to define a sort of lens to "peer" into the rest of your movie. Masks can be used without animation, but the really fun part is when you add animation to move the lens objects, revealing other parts of the underlying layers.

We'll return to masks and guide layers in detail later in this book when we explore animation in Part 6, "Animating with Flash Movies." But since we're investigating how layers are defined, we'll take a quick look at setting up Mask and Guide layers now.

Defining a Guide Layer

To change a layer to a Guide layer, select the layer in the Timeline, and choose **Modify**, **Layer** from the menu.

In the Layer Properties dialog box, click the **Guide** option button in the Type section, as shown in Figure 8.8.

Backstage Pass

Good Housekeeping Tips

It helps to assign names to your layers that help you keep track of the objects on them—like the sun, sky, monkey, trees, and ground layers back in Figure 8.7.

Naming layers will come in handy as you work with special types of layers in the next section of this chapter. You'll explore Guide layers and Mask layers, and you might well want to name your guide layer "Guide," and your mask layer "Mask."

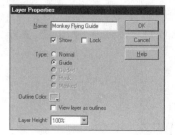

Figure 8.8

A Guide layer helps define motion in an movie.

Nitty Gritty Stuff

Guides Control Animation

We'll explore just *how* Guide layers are used to define animation in Chapter 16, "Automating Animation." For now, rest content knowing that you can create a Guide layer when you need one.

An example of a Guide layer is shown in Figure 8.9. The line in the Guide layer won't show when the movie is displayed, but will define motion for objects in the layer with which it is associated.

Figure 8.9

The Guide layer won't display in a Flash movie—it's only there to help define animation when we add additional frames.

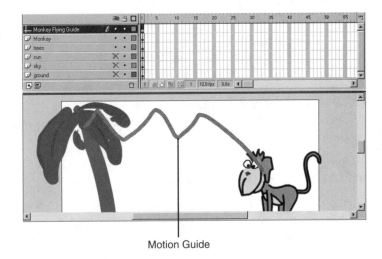

Motion Guide

Creating Peek Holes with Mask Layers

Mask layers act like the eye, nose, and mouth holes in a mask. They allow viewers to "see through" the Mask layer into layers below.

Objects on the mask layer define the mask. Mask objects can be any filled object (ovals, rectangles, or shapes).

Nitty Gritty Stuff

Some Objects Cannot Be Masks

Any filled shape can be a mask—if it's placed on a Mask layer. However, outlines cannot be used as mask objects. Nor can bitmap images.

After you define a Mask layer, you need to create (or assign existing layers to be) *masked* layers. These masked layers are layers that "show through" the holes in the Mask layer.

Nitty Gritty Stuff

Mask Versus Masked

How do you keep straight the difference between a Mask layer and a masked layer? Think about Zorro, the masked swordsman. He wore a mask that covered most of his face, revealing only his eyes. Similarly, a Mask layer covers other layers. And those masked layers are covered by a mask. OK, "High ho, Silver!" —oops, that's a different masked man.

When you create the mask, by default, it will take the layer bellow the Mask layer and automatically make it into a masked layer.

To define additional layers as masked layers, first select them. With your masked layer(s) selected, choose **Modify**, **Layer** and click the **Masked** option button in the Layer Properties dialog box.

Figure 8.10 shows a Mask layer on top of several other layers (the masked layers). The big white circle in the Mask layer will act as a "mask" when the movie is displayed.

Figure 8.10

When this movie is displayed, the big white circle will act as a mask, allowing viewers to see only *objects covered by the circle.*

You can view the effect of a Mask layer by locking the Mask layer. When the Mask layer is locked, Flash will reveal the effect of the mask, as shown in Figure 8.11.

Backstage Pass

Mask Colors

Flash guru (and our contributing artist) Paul Mickulecky tells me that he always makes his mask objects black so that they are easily visible when he unlocks the Mask layer. White may disappear on a white background. (If it's a black background then Paul says use white for the mask object.)

Figure 8.11

The image displayed in the movie is created by using the circle mask to display only part of underlying layers.

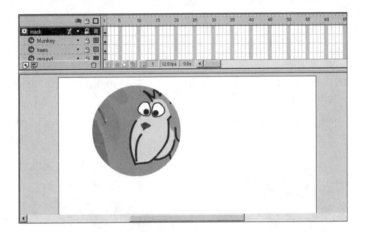

Backstage Pass

Good Housekeeping Tips

Another way to preview the effect of a mask is to lock all layers.

The Least You Need to Know

➤ Layers are the best way to handle objects that will be in front of or behind other objects.

➤ The icons next to each Layer name allow you to Show or Hide, Lock or Unlock layers, and to toggle between displaying layers as outlines, or as full images.

➤ You can cut, copy, and paste objects across layers.

➤ Guide layers don't appear in movies, but are useful for organizing multilayer images.

➤ Mask layers reveal only part of underlying Masked layer(s).

Write On: Making Text Flash-y

Most Web text can be boring. Sorry if I offended anyone, but face it: HTML keeps you from being very expressive with text.

With Flash, it's a different story. You can create text that tilts, stretches, skews, and morphs into shapes.

Text in a Flash

When you share text in a Flash movie, you get more precise control over how that text appears than if you tried to format text using HTML. Because visitors view your site through the Flash viewer embedded in their browsers, the cool attributes (like rotation) that you assign to text display on their Web pages just as you design it. I'll show you how to format text in this chapter.

What the Heck Is HTML?

HyperText Markup Language (HTML for short) is the minimalist language used by Web sites to communicate content to Web browsers. HTML itself is rather limited—and cannot, for example, display vector-based graphics like those you create in Flash. Modern browsers can display Flash files because they include the Flash viewer, opening up a whole new level of what can be conveyed in a Web site.

The space, rotation, color, and font attributes you assign to text will look fine in anyone's browser. However, the fonts you assign might not look the same in every browser. That's because font display in browsers depends on the fonts installed on your *visitor's* system.

If you apply a techie-looking Westminster font to your text, it might show up in a dreary Times Roman when viewed in a browser. There's a solution to that problem. I'll explain how you can make sure your fonts look the way you formatted them—on *any* browser—by converting text into shapes.

Wrapping It Down

To place text in a Flash movie, just click the **Text** tool in the Drawing toolbar. You can quickly select the Text tool by pressing T on your keyboard.

As you move your cursor over the Stage, the text cursor displays as an A with a crosshair attached. Click the Stage and type. A text box is created that expands to accommodate the text that you type (see Figure 9.1).

Figure 9.1

The Text tool displays as an A-shaped cursor. Click and type to add text, or draw a text box first to define text width.

Backstage Pass

Defining the Height and Width of a Text Box

If you want to define the width of a text box before you enter text, click and drag with the Text cursor to draw a text box. You aren't able to define the text box *height*, just the width. That's because the text box height expands to fit the text you type.

Select a block of text by clicking (just once) on it. When you select text with the Text tool, a single handle appears in the upper-right corner of the text box. You can click and drag that handle to change the width of the text box. As you adjust the width, your text rewraps to fill the box (see Figure 9.2). The size of the letters (the font size) stays the same when you adjust the size of the text box this way. If you're trying to make the text expand or shrink in size, skip ahead to the section "Scaling, Skewing, and Rotating Text."

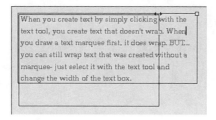

Figure 9.2

When text boxes are resized, text rewraps to fit the new text box width.

Twistin' & Turnin' Text

Resizing text boxes has no effect on the size, shape, or orientation of the actual text in the box. If the text box gets narrower, the box also gets longer. If the text box gets wider, the text box gets correspondingly shorter.

Figure 9.3

Viewing in a browser, this text has been scaled, rotated, and skewed.

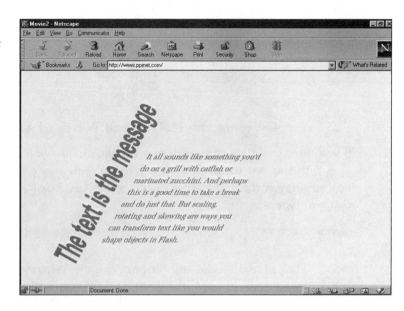

Scaling Text

Scaling text changes the actual shape of the text. Increasing the height when scaling text makes it taller and skinnier. Decreasing the height makes text short and squat. By scaling text, you have much more control over how it will look because you aren't limited to normal font sizes.

Nitty Gritty Stuff

What's the Difference Between Sizing and Scaling?

Earlier I explained that when you *resize* a text box, the font and font size stay the same. So, if you make a text box wider by *resizing* it, the text box gets *shorter*. Scaling is different. Scaling actually *distorts* the shape of the text. When you make a text box wider with *scaling*, it does not get shorter. Instead, the letters get fatter.

To scale text, select a text box with the Select tool (*not* the Text tool), and choose **Modify**, **Transform**, **Scale**. As soon as you do that, eight scaling handles appear on the corners and sides of the text box. Click and drag these handles to modify the size and shape of the text (see Figure 9.4).

Figure 9.4

Scaling text can make it fatter.

Backstage Pass

Maintaining Font Proportions While Scaling

One of the great things about scaling fonts in Flash is that you can stretch your fonts like a rubber band—making them wider or thinner as you change the font size. What if you want to *keep* the original proportions of the font? In that case, use the corner handles to change the scaling. Clicking and dragging corner handles resizes both height and width proportionally. If you are digitally inclined, you can choose **Modify**, **Transform**, **Rotate**, and **Scale** and change the size using a percentage.

Rotating Text

Like shapes, text boxes can be rotated. Select a text box using the Select (not the Text) tool. Choose **Modify**, **Transform**, **Rotate**. Click and drag any of the four round corner handles to rotate text (see Figure 9.5).

Figure 9.5

Rotating text.

Which Tool Selects Text?

The Text tool (the A in the toolbox) is used to select text when you want to edit the text. The Select tool (the arrow) is used to select text that you want to rotate, scale, or skew.

Skewing Text

Skewing distorts text blocks by tilting parallel sides of the box. Select the text box you want to skew with the Select tool, and choose **Modify**, **Transform**, **Rotate**. You'll see the same handles you see when you rotate text. (No wonder! You chose the same menu option!)

What Is Skewing?

Skewing is something like looking in a trick mirror at the county fair that makes you look like you're standing at an angle. The effect is created by offsetting parallel sides of a text box in opposite directions—for example, sliding the top of the box right, and the bottom of the box left.

With the rotation handles displayed, skew text by clicking and dragging one of the four *side* (not corner) handles of a text box (see Figure 9.6). You kind of have to experiment with this to get a feel for it, and when you do, you'll be hooked. Don't overdo it, but skewed text boxes enable you to do some fun things with text, such as making text display parallel to other objects on your page.

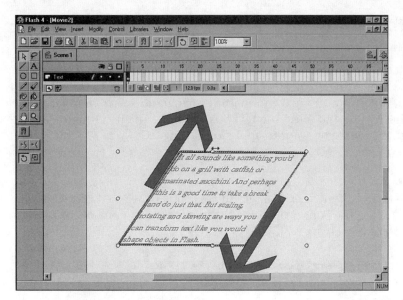

Figure 9.6
Skew text by clicking and dragging the side rotation handles.

Formatting Text

You can assign formatting to text in many ways in Flash 5. The Text menu provides quick and easy access to choosing text font, size, style, and alignment.

The Character/Paragraph/Text Options panel provides one-stop shopping for more complete control over how text is formatted in text boxes. You can activate these panels by choosing **Text**, **Paragraph**; **Text**, **Character**; or **Text**, **Options** from the menu.

Backstage Pass

Many Roads to the Text Panels

You can open the Character panel with the (Cmd-T) [Ctrl+T] keystroke shortcut. (Cmd-Shift-T) [Ctrl+Shift+T] opens the Paragraph options panel. And for the Windows inclined, you can access all three of the text panels by choosing **Window, Panels**.

Choosing Text to Format

The first step in formatting text is to select the text box to which you want to apply formatting changes.

If you want to make formatting changes to an *entire* text box, just click on the box with the Arrow tool. If you want to make formatting changes to *selected text* within a text box, first use the Text tool to select the text box, then use the text tool to click and drag to highlight the text you want to apply formatting to.

Changing Fonts

To apply changes to fonts or font sizes to a selected text box or selected text, choose **Text**, **Character**, and use the Font drop-down list to choose from one of the fonts installed on your system (see Figure 9.7).

Figure 9.7

Fonts and font sizes can be applied to selected text within a text box.

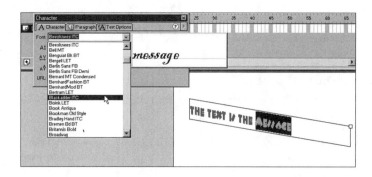

Will Visitors See My Fonts in Their Browser?

Not unless they have those fonts in their system. If the font you assign isn't available in a visitor's computer, Flash substitutes a close matching font. If you want to make sure your fonts display exactly as you create them, change them to shapes. (See the section "Text as Shapes," later in this chapter.)

A quick way to assign fonts to selected text is to choose **Text**, **Font** from the menu, and then choose a font from the pop-up menu. However, when you select fonts this way, you can't preview them before you assign them (as you can when you choose **Text**, **Character**) and use the Font drop-down list.

Sizing and Tracking Fonts

The Character panel allows you to define size for selected text both horizontally and vertically. The Font Height (vertical size) slider controls how high the text will be.

The Tracking slider (which sets the horizontal spacing between letters) is shown in Figure 9.8. This Tracking slider controls text spacing.

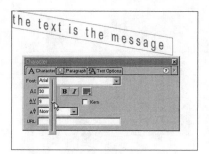

Figure 9.8

As you change Tracking (text spacing) using the sliders in the Character panel, your text spacing changes size on screen.

Kerning? Tracking?

My brand new, off-the-shelf version of Flash 5 comes with a Kerning check box in the Character panel. But this check box does not appear to change the way tracking is applied to text, and at this writing the support folks at Macromedia are confirming that this box doesn't do anything. Kerning is a typographic term for controlling the spacing between letters and words, and Flash's Tracking slider provides this kind of control over text.

If you want to fine tune horizontal spacing (tracking, kerning, whatever you call it), you can do so by selecting groups of two letters or characters, and applying specific kerning to those letters.

Setting Font Color

You can change font color for a selected text box or selected text by choosing a color from the Text (fill) Color icon in the Character panel.

You can also change the color of the text in a text box by selecting the text box and selecting fill color from the Color Area in the Toolbox.

When you select different characters, you can apply individual colors to those characters. This can be an effective tool for highlighting and creating effects with text. In Figure 9.9, I used different shades of gray to connote a message with my text.

Figure 9.9

You can't assign gradient fills to text blocks, but you can simulate the effect of a gradient by applying different shades and colors to individual letters.

Adding Font Style

The Character panel includes Bold (B) and Italic (I) icons. Click them to assign these font styles to selected text boxes or text.

Backstage Pass

Keystroke Shortcuts

Don't expect the familiar (Cmd-B) [Ctrl+B] or (Cmd-I) [Ctrl+I] to assign boldface and formatting in Flash. Those shortcuts might work in other Windows and Mac applications, but Flash marches to its own beat here. (Cmd-Shift-B) [Ctrl+Shift+B] applies boldface to selected text, and (Cmd-Shift-I) [Ctrl+Shift+I] applies italics.

Superscript/Subscript

Unlike kerning, superscript or subscript is always applied to selected letters. OK, it's technically possible to apply superscript or subscript to an entire text box, but there's no practical point to superscripting or subscripting *all* the text in a text box. The point is to elevate (superscript) or lower (subscript) some letters above or below the rest of the text. For example, the "nd" in 2nd Street is displayed as superscript.

To apply superscript or subscript to text, select the text within a text block using the Text tool, and choose either Superscript or Subscript from the Vertical Offset drop-down menu, as shown in Figure 9.10.

Figure 9.10

Superscript not only raises selected text, it applies a smaller-size font to the selected text.

Aligning and Spacing Paragraphs

Flash enables you to control paragraph attributes, including spacing between lines and alignment. Paragraphs can be aligned left, center, right, or full-justified (see Figure 9.11).

Figure 9.11

Paragraphs can be aligned left, centered, aligned right, or full justified.

The quickest way to align a paragraph is to select text, or a text box, and choose **Text, Align**, and select **Align Left**, **Align Center**, **Align Right**, or **Justify** from the menu.

You can also assign spacing to lines within an entire selected text box or to selected paragraphs. To assign paragraph spacing to a selected text box, or text, choose **Text, Paragraph**, and use the Line Spacing slider in the Paragraph panel to define spacing for a text box, or for selected lines of text, as shown in Figure 9.12.

Figure 9.12

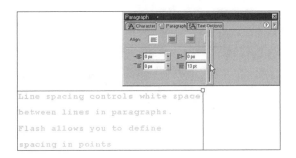

Line spacing controls white space between lines in paragraphs. Flash allows you to define spacing in points, instead of the usual Web measuring unit of screen pixels. In hardcopy printout, 72 points are an inch. Using points for line spacing is helpful because font sizes are defined in points.

Backstage Pass

Why Type When You Can Copy?

If you're like me (okay, even if you're not), you'd probably rather copy and paste a batch of text than type the text in. Many times the folks for whom you are developing a Flash movie will provide you with copy (text) to patch into the movie. Do that by first copying the text from the source document (Word, HTML pages, whatever). Then, draw a text box in Flash and paste the text into the box.

When text is simply pasted onto the stage (without creating a text box), the attributes of the pasted text are maintained as they were in your word processor. If you first create a text box thing and then paste text into the text box, the pasted text takes on the attributes of the text box (instead of the formatting it had in the word processor or other program).

Looks Good in Flash...But Will It Play in a Browser?

So far, you've explored plenty of formatting tricks that work in Flash. I guarantee you, when you test these text-formatting effects in a browser on your own computer, they'll look just as you defined them in Flash. How do I know that? Because I know that the fonts you assigned in Flash are on your computer, where they are available to your browser as well as Flash.

When folks with *different* font sets visit your Flash movie on a Web site, they might not have the fonts you applied to your text, and your movie will look different—sometimes awfully different—to them.

So all your hard work doesn't go unappreciated, you can guarantee that text appears just as you defined it, with all the kerning, skewing, and rotating intact, if you convert your text to shapes before publishing your movie.

Nitty Gritty Stuff

What Is Shape Text?

Technically speaking, after you convert text to a shape, it isn't text anymore. What was text becomes shapes. You can't use any of the Text options anymore—you can't assign boldface, italics, or paragraph alignment, for example. You can, however, use shape-editing techniques to change how the text looks.

The big downside of converting text to curves is that the size of the Flash file can dramatically increase in size. If you convert large blocks of text to curves, Flash has to store a lot of node information for each character. Converting large blocks of text to shapes can change a file from 10k, into a 100k memory hog.

Text as Shapes

To convert text to shapes, select a text box with the Arrow tool, and choose **Modify**, **Break Apart**. Your text is now a set of shapes. Not only is each letter a distinct shape, the dots on i's are distinct shapes as well.

After you've converted text to shapes, you not only ensure its display in movies on any operating system with any font set, you also open the door to all kinds of creativity with your text shapes (see Figure 9.13). Move 'em, rotate 'em, apply gradient fills: Everything that you can do to a shape you can now do to text shapes.

News Flash

After You Change Text to Shapes, It's Stuck

Don't expect to do any text editing after you convert your text to shapes. If you expect to do that, make a copy of your text box and save it for future editing *before* you convert the text to shapes.

Figure 9.13

Fun with shaped text.

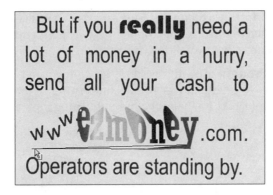

Convert Some Text to Shapes

What if you want to convert *some* of your text to a shape, but not all of it? You cannot convert part of a text box to shapes; you have to convert the entire text box.

The only way to convert some text is to create more than one text box and convert one or more of your text boxes to shapes.

The Least You Need to Know

➤ You can apply formatting to change the size, font, color, and paragraph properties of text.

➤ Click a text box with the Text tool and use the formatting features in the Text Character panel to define font, font size, and font color.

➤ Use the Paragraph panel to define paragraph alignment and line spacing.

➤ Click and drag within a text box to apply formatting to just the *selected* type.

Part 4

Hanging Out at the Recycling Center

Flash movies require many objects that are used over and over again. Flash has a very efficient and easy to use technique for storing these objects. In the following chapters, you'll learn to package objects as symbols that will be repeated in movies

You'll also learn to use Flash's library of existing symbols, and stash your own symbols in the Flash library as well.

Recycling with Symbols

In This Chapter

➤ Creating reusable symbols

➤ Placing symbols in movies

➤ Changing how a symbol looks throughout a movie

➤ Customizing how individual *instances* of a symbol appear in a movie

---

Graphics objects have a big limitation: they can only be used once. Symbols, on the other hand, can be used over and over again.

Storing Objects as Symbols

There are two main advantages to saving graphics objects as symbols:

➤ Symbols cut down on file size.

➤ Symbols are easier to use and edit *throughout* a movie.

Let's use the aquarium scene in Figure 10.1 to illustrate how this works. The entire scene is made up of *five* Symbols. Each of these Symbols can be used (and in most cases *is* used) more than once. When additional frames are added to the movie, and the fish start "swimming" around, the same Symbols can be used in different locations throughout the movie.

Figure 10.1

The Symbol library on the right displays the five Symbols that make up the drawing on the Stage. Each of these Symbols can be reused in any frame. Note that the fish Symbol appears in different sizes within the drawing.

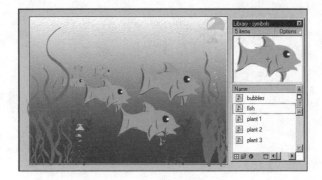

When a Symbol is used, it's called an *instance*. Instances of a Symbol can be modified—rotated, reshaped, recolored, and so on.

Symbols Versus Copy and Paste

Couldn't you just reuse graphics objects by copying and pasting them in different frames? Yes, you can do that. But you lose the two valuable attributes that you get with Symbols: you don't conserve file size, and you can't easily edit a drawing *throughout* a movie.

Creating Graphics Symbols

To create a new Symbol, choose **Insert**, **New Symbol** from the menu bar. The Symbol Properties dialog box appears, as shown in Figure 10.2.

Figure 10.2

When you create a new Symbol, assign a name that will help you remember what graphics it contains.

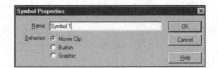

The Symbol Properties dialog box lets you choose a name for your Symbol, and also prompts you to choose between a graphic, a button, or a movie clip Symbol. If you are creating a graphic (and in this example, you are!), choose **Graphic**.

After you click **OK** in the Symbol Properties dialog box, it might appear like nothing much has happened. The Stage will look like it always does. But above the Layers list, you'll see an icon indicating that you are editing a Symbol.

Creating New Symbols

Just to be clear, right now we're talking about creating a *brand new* symbol from scratch. Later in this chapter, I'll show you how to convert an existing graphic object into a symbol (see "Converting Objects to Symbols").

Those Other Symbols

Buttons are interactive objects that react when a visitor hovers over them or clicks on them. Chapter 12, "Creating Control Buttons," discusses how to create buttons. Movie clips are entire chunks of an animated movie. You can also use the Symbol Properties dialog box to create Symbols of these types.

Draw a Symbol just as you would create any other drawing. Don't worry about grouping objects (unless it helps you with your drawing)—Symbols act like grouped objects. And don't worry about the location of your Symbol on the Stage. You'll deal with that when you return to your movie.

Figure 10.3 shows a Symbol being edited in Symbol view.

Figure 10.3

The Fish icon indicates that you are editing a Symbol. Clicking on the Scene 1 button to the left of the active Symbol icon returns you to regular editing mode.

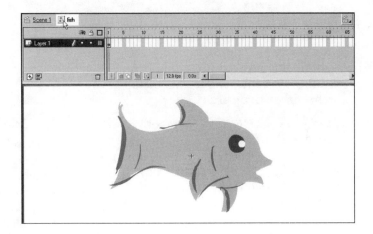

Where's My Drawing???

When you return to regular editing mode, the Symbol you created is not yet visible. Don't worry, it's safely stored in the Library. Choose **Window**, **Library** from the menu bar to see a list of all your Symbols. Later in this chapter I'll explain how to use (and reuse) these Symbols.

After you finish your Symbol, choose **Edit**, **Edit Movie** to return to regular editing mode.

Converting Existing Objects into Symbols

You can also convert an existing drawing into a Symbol. To do that, select the objects that you will convert into a symbol (using the Arrow or Lasso tools). Then, after selecting *all* of the objects that you want included, choose **Insert**, **Convert to Symbol**. The Symbol Properties dialog box appears. Enter a name for your Symbol in the Name dialog box, and click OK.

Placing Symbols in Movies

To see your Symbols, choose **Window**, **Library**. The Library opens to display Symbols created for the open movie.

After you've created one or more Symbols, you can place them on the Stage—over and over again. Do this by click-dragging a Symbol onto the Stage, as shown in Figure 10.4.

130

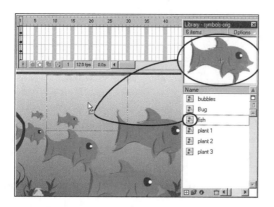

Figure 10.4

You can drag a symbol from the Library into a movie by dragging the preview picture at the top of the library, the icon next to the symbol name, or the symbol name itself onto the stage.

Looking at Symbols

Complex movies are made up of many symbols. Flash designers rely on symbols because they drastically reduce file size (since they can be reused in frame after frame in a movie). Further, when you start to animate your movie with generated motion between frames, Flash requires that you use symbols for automated animation.

With all this emphasis on symbols, it's worth taking a minute (or a page) to walk through how to organize your symbols.

The Symbol Library

The Library window displays a list of Symbols that were created for your open movie. You can change the way these Symbols are displayed, and you can use the Library window to help find Symbols in a hurry after you build up a nice big library of them.

When you click on a Symbol in the Name area (the bottom half of the Library window), that Symbol displays in the top half of the window.

The scrollbar on the right side of the window allows you to scroll up and down long lists of Symbols. The three icons on the right side of the dialog box are shown in Figure 10.5, and allow you to change how the Symbol list displays.

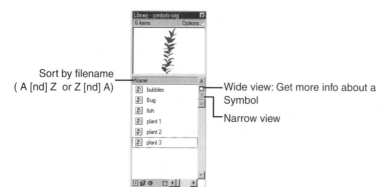

Sort by filename
(A [nd] Z or Z [nd] A)

Wide view: Get more info about a Symbol

Narrow view

Figure 10.5

You can sort file names A–Z or Z–A in the Library window, and you can toggle between a wide display (that includes info about the Symbol) or narrow view (seen in this figure).

131

Backstage Pass

A Trip to the Library Is Coming Up

Libraries can store all kinds of objects so things can quickly get rather complex. In Chapter 11, "Building Your Own Library" you'll explore how to manage all kinds of libraries in more detail. Here, I'll explain just enough to help you find and use Symbols for this chapter's purposes.

Spotting Symbols on the Stage

When you select a Symbol on the Stage, the Symbol appears with a diagonal-line bounding box like the ones that appear around a grouped object.

To help you figure out that you have selected a Symbol, Flash also displays a crosshair in the middle of the Symbol, as shown in Figure 10.6.

Figure 10.6

The fish are Symbols; the bubbles are not. Selected Symbols display with a crosshair symbol in the middle of them, whereas other selected objects (even grouped objects) don't display the + sign when selected

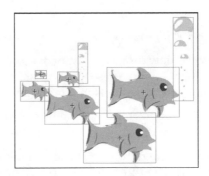

Using Symbols in Movies

One of the really cool things about Symbols is that after you use them, you can globally modify them. For example, if you design a red fish, and you want to turn him (or her) green, you simply change the Symbol, and *all instances* of the fish turn from red to green.

Changing Symbols

An easy way to edit a Symbol is to click the Symbol name in the bottom part of the Symbol library window, and then double-click on the picture that displays in the top half of the window.

After you open a Symbol in Symbol mode, you can edit it to your heart's content. All of the drawing attributes discussed in Chapters 3 through 6 (lines, fills, scale, rotation, and so on) can be changed in Symbol mode.

After you make changes to a Symbol, choose **Edit**, **Edit Movie** to return to your movie. Any changes you made to your Symbol will be saved, and the Symbol library will show those changes.

And...any change you made to a Symbol will be applied to *every instance* of that Symbol. How's that for quick graphics editing?

Another Way to Edit Symbols

Another way to edit a Symbol is to click on an instance of the Symbol in a movie, and then choose **Edit, Edit Symbols** from the menu bar.

Or...to make things even more convenient, you can edit *just one instance* of a Symbol.

Changing Symbol Instances

Some attributes of an individual instance of a Symbol can be edited right on the Stage. You can scale, rotate, and move instances of Symbols. When you edit a single instance of a Symbol, *only that instance* is affected.

So, for example, if you rotate an instance of a Symbol of a fish, only that one fish gets rotated, all other instances of a Symbol stay the same.

You cannot, however, change the fill (or outline) of a single instance of a Symbol by using the Ink Bottle or Paint Bucket tools.

You *can* modify the fill coloring of an *instance* of a Symbol. It's just a little more complicated than using the Paint Bucket tool. To modify the coloring of a single instance of a

From Symbol to Object

If you want use the Ink Bottle or Paint Bucket tools to change the fill and outline of a Symbol, you can select the Symbol and choose **Modify, Break Apart**. After you do this, you can modify anything about an object, but it is no longer a Symbol instance, it's just a regular ol' drawing object.

Symbol, click on the *instance* of the Symbol on the Stage, and choose **Modify, Instance** (Ctrl+I (CMD+I for Mac). This opens the Instance panel. Click the **Effect** tab in the Instance panel to open the Effect panel. This is where you modify the color and other properties of a single symbol instance.

To change the color of an instance, choose Tint from the drop-down menu in the **Effect** panel. Use the tint color palette or mixer to choose a new color for the selected instance, as shown in Figure 10.7.

Figure 10.7

Choosing a tint alters the color of a single selected instance of a symbol

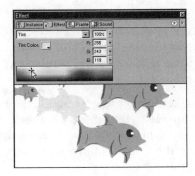

Altering tint is only one of the five options in the Effects panel that you can use to change how a selected symbol instance is colored. The whole list follows:

➤ **None**—Returns an instance to the fill coloring assigned to the Symbol.

➤ **Brightness**—Lets you darken or lighten an instance. Higher values in the Brightness slider lighten the color of an instance; lower values darken the color.

➤ **Tint**—Allows you to choose a new color by clicking in the color space, entering RGB (Red, Green, Blue) values, or choosing a color from the pop-up color palette. After you choose a color, use the Tint slider to define how thoroughly you want to apply the color to the Symbol instance.

➤ **Alpha**—Displays a slider that allows you to make an instance more or less transparent. Increase transparency by choosing a lower Alpha percentage value. A value of 0% will turn an instance completely transparent.

➤ **Advanced**—Doesn't give you any new options, but it allows you to define color and transparency (Alpha) for an instance all at once, as shown in Figure 10.8.

Figure 10.8

The Advanced option in the Effects panel allows you to set both color (using either percentages of red, green, and blue, or standard RGB coloring values) as well as transparency (Alpha values).

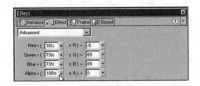

The Least You Need to Know

➤ Symbols are reusable graphic objects.

➤ Symbols are displayed in the Library Window.

➤ You can place Symbols in a movie by dragging them from the Library Window onto the Stage.

➤ Each time you use a Symbol in a movie, you place an *instance* of that Symbol.

➤ Changes to Symbols are applied *globally*, to all instances of the Symbol.

➤ Individual instances of a Symbol can be moved, resized, rotated, and have their fill color adjusted.

Building Your Own Library

In This Chapter

➤ Using Flash's clip art libraries

➤ Keeping track of your symbols

➤ Organizing symbols

➤ Borrowing symbols from other movies

➤ Replacing symbols throughout a movie

After you accumulate a roster of Symbols, you'll want to get more control over them than just being able to drag them into a movie. Flash lets you sort Symbols, organize your Symbols into easy-to-find folders, and even send them from one movie to another.

Keeping Actors on Call

In Chapter 10, "Recycling with Symbols," you discovered how Symbols are a potent tool for organizing and deploying graphics objects. After you pile up a bunch of these handy things, you'll want to organize them. The Library window has many of the features of a file manager, and it can help you sort and find the Symbols you need. It can even help you replace one Symbol with another throughout an entire movie.

With Flash 5, you can easily integrate symbol libraries from one movie into another movie. So when your animated mega-hit "Creatures in My Aquarium" gets recycled as "Creatures in My Aquarium II," you can pull all the lovable characters from Movie I and drop them right into the sequel.

Flash's Pre-Fab Libraries

Along with symbols that you create for your movie, Flash comes with six "common libraries." Back in the day, we used to call these pre-fab collections of artwork clip art, but now that we're all into multimedia, Flash calls them libraries.

Choose **Window, Common Libraries** to display a flyout menu with the six common libraries. The Graphics common library has a modest selection of clip art that you can use just like symbols you create yourself. Figure 11.1 shows symbols being dragged onto the Stage.

Figure 11.1

Flash's libraries are basically a selection of clip art. Instances of them can be modified, but the Symbols themselves can't be edited or deleted from the library.

Backstage Pass

Button, Movie, and Sound Clip Art Files

The Buttons (and Advanced Buttons) libraries have pre-made buttons that react to being clicked—you'll explore buttons in Chapter 12, "Creating Control Buttons." Movie Clips are little animations—moving objects—that can be plugged into movies. Sounds are files that can be used for movie soundtracks—you'll check that out in Chapter 18, "Crank It Up!"

You can open all of the Flash clip art libraries at once if you really want to. As you open them, they pile up on each other, and you can't tell how many library windows you have open. You can move them by clicking and dragging on the title bar of each library window, as shown in Figure 11.2.

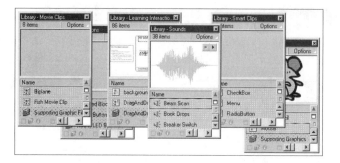

Figure 11.2

Too many library windows! A click on the Close button (x) will close them one at a time. On Macintosh computers, the close window button is in the top left of the window.

Organizing Libraries

When you create your first Symbol, you initiate a library associated with the open movie. That library can be used with other movies, but every movie with Symbols has its own library, and every library (except for the clip art ones) is associated with a movie.

Because your library might end up with lots of Symbols, it will be helpful to clean it up and organize it periodically. Oh, you're not the type who likes to clean and organize? Neither an I, but Flash makes it easy to keep your Symbols organized, and an organized Symbol library can make the work of putting a movie together much easier. Remember, you're not organizing your library because you're particularly tidy; you're doing it because you want to maximize fun and minimize work when you put your movie together.

Scoping Out Your Symbols

For serious Symbol management, you'll want to display your Symbol library in wide view. Do that by clicking and dragging on the edges of the Symbol library, or just click on the Wide View icon to the right of the first Symbol name.

In Wide view, you can see detailed information about your Symbols. In Figure 11.3, you can see the Name, Kind, Use Count, and Date Modified (last) for each Symbol in the movie library.

Nitty Gritty Stuff

Organizing Clip Art Libraries

The pre-fab Flash libraries are organized into folders. Flash has tools for reorganizing these folders, but they don't work with the common libraries. You can, however, organize the Symbol library containing your own Symbols into folders.

Backstage Pass

Sharing Symbols

There are ways to get Symbols from one movie into the library of another movie. The easiest way is to copy a Symbol from one movie into another movie, and then save it as a Symbol in the new movie.

Figure 11.3

You can sort the symbol library by clicking at the top of a column, and clicking the Sort icon. Clicking the Sort icon a second time toggles between sorting A-Z, and Z-A (or higher values first and lower values first).

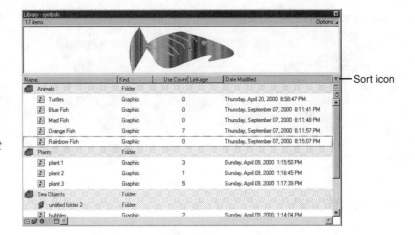

The name of a Symbol can be modified by double-clicking on it and typing in a new name. The Kind column tells you whether the Symbol is a graphic, animation (movie), button, or sound.

The Use Count column is kind of cool. It tells you how many times a Symbol is used in your movie. To update the count, click on the Options pop-up menu in the Symbol Library window, and make sure the Keep Count Updated option is checked, as shown in Figure 11.4.

Figure 11.4

Flash updates the count of how many times a Symbol is used in a movie only if the Keep Use Counts Updated option is checked.

Creating Folders

When you accumulate a big list of Symbols in a library, you can organize them into folders. Since many movies will have dozens, or even hundreds of symbols, organizing these guys into folders will make it much easier to find them when you need them.

140

Nitty Gritty Stuff

Linkage

The Linkage column in the Library panel notes whether a symbol is linked to a file on at a URL (a Web location). Linkages can be used to embed symbols that are automatically updated when the URL file changes.

Create a new folder by clicking on the Options pop-up menu in the Library-symbols window, and choosing **Options**, **New Folder**.

After you create a new folder, you can type a folder name, as shown in Figure 11.5.

Figure 11.5

When you create a folder, you get prompted to name it. Don't agonize too long over a name; you can always rename a folder by double-clicking on the folder name and entering a new name.

After you set up the folder, you can drag Symbols into it in the Library-Symbols window by just clicking and dragging (see Figure 11.6).

Other helpful organizing tools are found in the **Options** pop-up menu in the Library-Symbols window:

➤ **New Symbol**—Creates a new (blank) Symbol space in the Library-Symbols window. You need to choose **Edit** (later down the menu) to actually create a Symbol.

➤ **New Folder**—Creates a new folder—duh. You might think that if you already have a folder selected, this option creates a subfolder. That works only if you have a symbol or subfolder selected. Otherwise, create a new folder, and drag it into an existing folder.

141

Figure 11.6

The Red Fish Symbol is being dragged into the Animals folder, where she will be easy to find when you need her.

➤ **Rename**—Lets you change the name of a Symbol (or folder).

➤ **Move to New Folder**—Another way to get a Symbol out of one folder and into another (clicking and dragging is easier).

➤ **Duplicate**—The most useful feature in this menu—it creates a new Symbol that is a copy of the selected Symbol. Edit the new Symbol for a variant of your original Symbol.

➤ **Properties**—Lets you rename a button, or edit it.

The rest of the options are pretty self-explanatory.

Sharing Libraries Between Movies

If you want to have access to an entire Symbol library from another movie, choose **File**, **Open as Library** from the menu bar, and double-click on a Flash movie in the Open as Library dialog box.

Serious Symbolism

Symbols are hard to keep track of in large movies. To help you out, Flash comes armed with something called the Object Inspector that tells you what a Symbol is.

You can also use Flash to search out all instances of a Symbol in a movie, and substitute another Symbol.

ID'ing Symbols with the Info Panel

To ID a symbol on the Stage, first select it, then click on the Show Info icon in the Status Bar, as shown in Figure 11.7.

How Many Symbol Libraries Can You Open?

You can open as many Symbol libraries as you want. One trick for keeping Symbols organized is to create Symbol libraries for blank movies. In this way, you can build up sets of Symbols that can be used in any movie. They are technically Symbol sets for a movie, but really they are just collections of Symbols you can use anywhere.

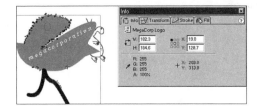

Figure 11.7

Show Info tells you the exact coordinates of a Symbol instance on the Stage (X being vertical location, Y being horizontal) as well as the height and width of the instance. The Use Center Point check box turns the center of the instance into the locator point for the X and Y distances (measured from the upper-left corner of the Stage).

Using a Library to Switch Symbols

Scenario: Your startup has just been acquired by a megacorporation and the old company logo needs to get replaced by the new corporate logo. Ordinarily this would be a time-consuming task consisting of locating each instance of an image and manually replacing it with the new one. Not so with Flash!

You can switch one Symbol for another in Flash. Here's how:

Showing Info

Clicking on the Show Info icon a second time hides the Show Info panel. You can also quickly activate (or hide) Show Info by pressing (Cmd+Option+I)[Ctrl+Alt+I].

1. On the Stage, use the Arrow tool to click on the Symbol to be replaced.

2. Choose **Modify, Instance** (Cmd+I) [Ctrl+I] to open the Instance panel, as shown in Figure 11.8.

Figure 11.8

Garage Logo is about to be replaced throughout the movie by MegaCorp logo. The Switch Symbols icon will become active after a replacement Symbol is selected.

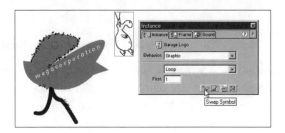

3. Click on the Swap Symbol icon to open the Swap Symbol dialog box. In the Swap Symbol dialog box, click on the symbol that will replace the selected symbol. When you click OK, the selected symbol replaces the original symbol.

Backstage Pass

Search and Replace Symbols

If you want to change all instances of a symbol, simply edit the symbol. You can do that easily by double-clicking on a symbol instance, and making changes in the Symbol window.

Then, choose **Edit**, **Edit Movie** to return to the movie editing window.

The Least You Need to Know

➤ Symbols created in a movie are automatically placed in a Symbol library for that movie.

➤ Every movie has one Symbol library of its own. Other Symbol libraries come with Flash (clip art), or can be opened from other movies.

➤ Symbol libraries can be sorted by Symbol name, how often the Symbol has been used, or the date the Symbol was created.

➤ You can edit a Symbol, and the change is reflected throughout a movie.

Part 5

Getting Your Buttons Pushed

Flash is great for creating interactive objects—things that do things when clicked. Like control buttons that blink, make sounds, or jump to new Web pages when clicked.

In the following chapters, you'll learn to design buttons that accept what the techies call "user input"—when someone clicks, they do something. You'll also learn to collect information from people watching your movie, and then use that information to customize their movie experience.

OOOH...

Creating Control Buttons

In This Chapter

➤ How buttons work in Flash movies

➤ Using Flash's button clip art

➤ Creating buttons from scratch

➤ Defining a clickable area for a button

The first half (or so) of this book covered the basic drawing tools needed to create graphics objects in Flash. *Buttons* are objects that react when "touched" by a mouse. They are different from the objects you've explored in earlier chapters in that they *do* something.

Preparing Buttons for Web Pages

Buttons are essential elements of Flash movies, and especially movies intended for Web sites. Folks expect to go to a Web site, and click on a button to make something happen. That something might be getting transported to another Web page, hearing a sound, or launching a movie.

Buttons stick out at Web sites because when you *hover* over them (move your mouse on top of them without clicking), or click on them, they change.

In the Web site in Figure 12.1, the buttons in the Flash animation display a dot next to them when hovered over.

Figure 12.1

By changing when hovered over, buttons in this Web site provide an interactive feel, and make it obvious that the visitor is selecting something when he or she clicks.

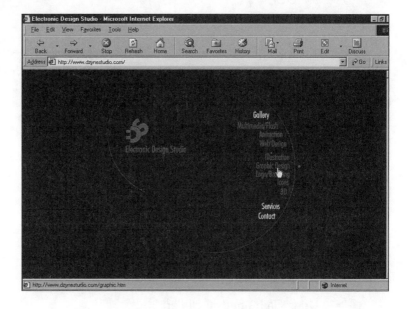

In Flash, basic buttons have three possible *events* that trigger changes in how the button looks: Up, Over, and Down. A fourth state—Hit—does not display.

➤ The **Up** state is how the button looks before anyone clicks on it.

➤ The **Over** state is how the button looks when a mouse cursor hovers over the button without clicking.

➤ The **Down** state is how the button looks when it is clicked on with a mouse.

➤ The **Hit** state is actually just a placeholder for the button. It does not display in a movie.

Not all buttons have to have all four states defined, and some buttons have even more states, but these are the basic four states that most buttons use.

Figure 11.2 shows a button in its up...and its down state.

Figure 12.2

In its down state, this clip art button from Flash rotates counter-clockwise.

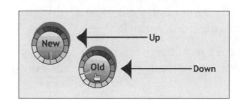

Events and States

The terms *event* and *state* describe things that a visitor can do to a button. For example, when a visitor moves his or her cursor *over* a button, that is an event. The *over* state that you define for a button defines how a button will react to that event. The *up* state defines how a button reactions when there are *no events*—when a mouse is not pointing to or clicking on a button. The other event that can happen to a button is for a visitor to click on it. The *down* state defines what happens when a visitor *clicks* on a button.

Creating Buttons with the Button Library

The easiest way to create buttons is to cop one from the clip art selections in the Button Library that comes with Flash.

Using Symbol Buttons

To use one of the buttons in the Symbol library, choose **Window**, **Common Libraries**, **Buttons**.

You can see all the states of a button Symbol in the Library window by clicking on the Play arrow in the Library, as shown in Figure 12.3.

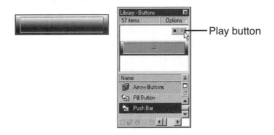

Play button

Figure 12.3

Clicking on the Play arrow in the Library window cycles a button through all three states: Up displays before you click the Play button. When you click the Play button, you see the Over, Down, and Hit states.

After previewing how a button will look, you can drag it out of the Library window and onto the Stage.

Editing Symbol Instances

Buttons can be edited on the Stage—you can scale them, rotate them, and add text on top of them.

Normally, buttons need some kind of text—or at least a Symbol—so that folks know what they are clicking! You can place text next to a button (refer to Figure 12.1), or right on top of a button (refer to Figure 12.2).

To test buttons on the Stage, choose **Control**, **Enable Simple Buttons** from the menu bar. With buttons enabled, you can click on buttons and test effects right on the Stage. But you can't edit buttons with the Enable Buttons feature selected. So before you try to add text to a button, make sure this feature is not selected.

Editing Button Symbols

When you edit a button on the Stage, technically you are creating an instance of a button Symbol. Chapter 10, "Recycling with Symbols," discusses Symbols and instances in detail.

Building a Button from Scratch

Creating a button from scratch actually involves creating a mini-animated movie. The first frame in the movie is the button before it is hovered over or clicked on. The second frame displays the button as it looks when a mouse hovers over it. The third frame shows the button when it is clicked. The fourth frame defines the clickable area of a button.

A Super-Quick Look at Frames

We'll explore frames in more detail when we look at creating animated movies. But for now, just note that frames are the rectangles in a movie (or symbol) timeline.

You select a frame by clicking on it with your mouse. When you select a frame, you can edit the contents of that frame in the stage.

Buttons are a special type of movie that have four frames. Each of these frames can be clicked, and edited. With that as your quick intro to frames, let's look at how to use them to create a button.

Creating a Four-Frame Button Movie

To create a new button, follow these steps:

1. With a movie open, choose **Insert**, **New Symbol**.
2. In the Symbol Properties dialog box, enter a name for your button, and click the Button options button for the type of Behavior, as shown in Figure 12.4. When you click OK, you open the Symbol Editing view.

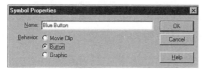

Figure 12.4

By choosing the Button option, you are generating a four-frame movie.

3. In Symbol editing view, draw a shape that will be the Up state of your button, before anyone clicks on it or hovers over it. Figure 12.5 shows a basic button shape.

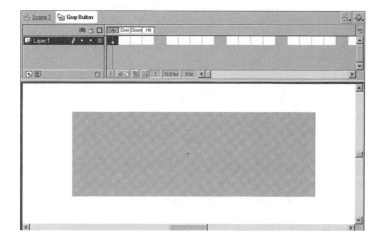

Figure 12.5

It's best not to include text when you design a button. You can add text to specific instances of your button Symbol later. Note: This button is magnified to 400%—most buttons don't fill the entire stage at 100% zoom!

4. In order to add the second button frame for the Over state, click in the Over Frame, as shown in Figure 12.6. With Frame 2 selected, choose **Insert**, **Keyframe** (to duplicate the previous frame), or **Insert**, **Blank Keyframe** (to edit the frame from scratch). Create the "Over" version of your button that will display when a mouse cursor moves over the button.

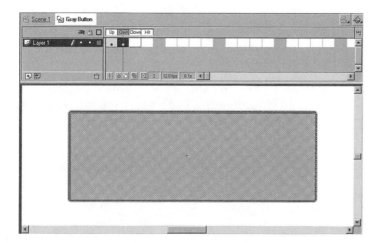

Figure 12.6

The second ("Over") frame in the button window is used to design a button as it appears when a visitor moves his or her mouse over the button in a movie.

151

Nitty Gritty Stuff

Keyframes

You might note that as you create content for frames, the frame appears with a black circle in the Timeline. This indicates that the frame is a Keyframe. *Keyframes* are frames in an animation that have content. You'll explore keyframes, and how they relate to other kinds of frames, in Chapter 15, "Everybody Dance Now!"

5. To create the "Down" button, click on the Down frame, and choose **Insert**, **Keyframe**, or **Insert**, **Blank Keyframe**. Design a third version of the button that will display when the button is clicked.

6. The final step in creating a button is to define the "Hit" state. Do this by selecting the Hit frame, and again choosing **Insert**, **Keyframe** or **Insert**, **Blank Keyframe**. Then draw a shape (usually a rectangle or oval) that defines the clickable area for the button. This area should be *at least* large enough to cover the three previous buttons, so that when a visitor clicks on them, they are activating the button.

News Flash

Hit State Matters

If you don't have a Hit state shape, the shape of the object in the Down state frame will be the default Hit state.

Editing a Button

Buttons take trial-and-error to create. You will want to make 'em, test 'em, and fix 'em. And repeat that process many times. (Welcome to the world of Web graphics design.)

Here's a quick summary of how to test and edit a button:

➤ Test a button by dragging it from the Library window onto the Stage. You can test a button by choosing **Control**, **Enable Buttons**, or by choosing **Control**, **Test Movie**. If you use the Test Movie option, close the Test Movie window by clicking on the Close button after you test your button.

➤ Edit a button by clicking on it in the Library window, and choosing Edit from the Options pop-up menu at the top of the library. Change your button in Symbol editing mode by making changes to any of the four frames that comprise the Symbol.

After you edit your button, choose **Edit**, **Edit Movie** to return to normal editing mode. Any changes you made to your button will be applied to all instances of the button in your movie.

Testing the Hit Frame

Remember, buttons have *four* frames: The Up, Over, and Down frames define how a button looks when it's just sitting there, when you hover over it, or when you click "down" on it. Okay, that's three frames. How do you test the Hit frame?

The Hit frame defines the clickable area for a button—the area of the button that responds to being clicked.

Figure 12.7 shows a button in both the Down and the Over states.

Figure 12.7

The Hit area for this button extends beyond the area covered by the graphics that is used for the Up state.

As you can see in Figure 12.7, the hand icon appears when a visitor hovers over not just the button itself, but the area to the right of the button, where a dark dot appears. In order for the dark dot to be included in the clickable area, the Hit Area must extend to encompass that area.

The easiest way to adjust the size of the hit frame in relation to other frames is to turn on the *Onion Skin* feature for all four frames. Do this by selecting all four button frames and clicking on the Onion Skin or Onion Skin Outlines icon, as shown in Figure 12.8

With Onion Skin Outlines turned on, you can locate objects within (or outside) the hit area.

A Quick Intro to Onion Skinning

Onion skinning allows you to see the contents of more than one frame at a time. This is helpful in aligning objects in the four states of a button symbol window.

Figure 12.8

Turning on Onion Skin makes the frames in a layer semi-transparent, so you can see through them to locate objects in relation to their location in other frames. Onion Skin outlines displays other frames without fills. Here, you can see that the Hit state shape is larger than the other button shapes.

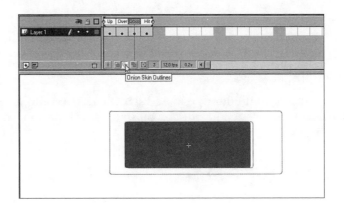

Backstage Pass

What Happens When You Click a Button?

In this chapter, you've explored the process of creating buttons that respond to mouse events by changing their look and shape. But buttons normally have other actions assigned to them as well, like serving as links to Web sites. Assigning actions to buttons is covered in Chapter 13, "Interacting with the Audience."

The Least You Need to Know

➤ Buttons are special Symbols that respond to mouse events.

➤ Buttons respond to three different mouse events—Up (not touched by a mouse), Over (having a mouse point to them, but not clicked), and Down (clicked on).

➤ Buttons are composed by creating a new Symbol, and choosing the Button option in the Symbol Properties dialog box.

➤ The Hit frame of the Mouse Symbol defines the clickable area for a button.

SO, WHERE ARE YOU FOLKS FROM?!

Interacting with the Audience

In This Chapter

➤ Making movies interactive

➤ Allowing the viewer to freeze the action

➤ Providing links to frames

➤ Providing links to Web pages

In Chapter 1 of this book, you explored the basic way Flash presents movies: Each frame in a movie displays in sequence: 1, 2, 3…and so on. In this way, you can arrange frames to display animation, or you can simply have different frames present different information, like with a slide show.

Now it's time to add a twist to that routine—you can use buttons to allow users to interact with your movie.

As we add actions to buttons, you'll be introduced to Flash's action script. Flash 5 uses a significantly different scripting language than Flash 4—the new version is similar to JavaScript. But don't worry, none of that matters to us because Flash allows us to generate its new Action Script code by making easy-to-follow menu choices.

What About Actions from Flash 4 Movies?

If you created a movie in Flash 4 and assigned actions to buttons, your action scripts will be converted to the new version of Action Script when you open your movie file in Flash 5.

Assigning Actions to Flash Buttons

In the previous chapter, you created some cute little buttons. How about you make them do something?

You can assign properties to a button so that it will allow a visitor to stop your movie when he or she sees something particularly interesting, and start it up again when they're ready for more. You can also set up buttons that visitors can use to jump to the frame in your movie that they are interested in. You can even create buttons in your Flash movie that let visitors jump to a different Web site.

Figure 13.1 shows a Flash frame displayed in a Web browser. The buttons in the frame allow visitors to control the movie.

Figure 13.1

The Contact Us button is linked to a frame that provides contact information, allowing a visitor to control the flow of the movie.

The following steps outline the basic process of assigning an action to a button. The rest of this chapter will explain exactly how to make those actions do what you want your button to do.

Skip the Flash Animation?

Many Web sites open with a Flash movie—either an animated show, or a series of slides that present information. Cool as these opening presentations are, sometimes visitors will want to skip them—like if they're already been to your site 2,807 times. Many Flash animations offer a button that allows a visitor to skip the animation and jump right to the final frame, or to a Web site.

1. Place a button on the Stage. You can create a new button (refer back to chapter 12, "Creating Control Buttons.") Or, you can use one of Flash's buttons by choosing **Window**, **Common Libraries**, **Buttons**, and then drag one of the buttons onto the stage.

2. Select the button with the Arrow tool, and choose **Modify**, **Instance** from the menu bar.

3. In the Instance Panel, click on the Edit Actions icon, as shown in Figure 13.2. The Object Actions panel appears.

Figure 13.2

Button actions can include jumping around within a movie, triggering a sound effect, or jumping to a Web site.

4. In the Object Actions panel, click **Basic Actions** to display the available actions, as shown in Figure 13.3.

5. If you are assigning an action to a mouse click, select OnMouseEvent. The rest of this chapter will explain how to choose Mouse events, and how to assign actions to them.

157

Figure 13.3

You can get a description of an action by hovering over the command and reading the mouse tip.

Defining Mouse Events for Actions

Assigning an *action* to a button (like "skip to Frame 4," for example) involves two steps: figuring out what *event* will trigger the action, and figuring out what action to assign to that event.

> ### What Kinds of Events Do Mice Have, Anyway?
>
> A mouse event means something that a visitor does to a button with or to his or her mouse, like moving over the button, or clicking on it. You'll explore all possible mouse events in the next section of this chapter.

You can choose from seven different events to associate with an action. After you go through the five-step process at the beginning of this chapter, you are prompted with a set of check boxes that allow you to choose what mouse event to associate with the selected button. The options, (plus an eighth checkbox that allows you to assign a key stroke to activate the mouse event) appear on the bottom of the Object Actions panel, as shown in Figure 13.4.

The possible mouse events are (drum roll please...)

➤ **Press**—Clicking on the button with the mouse triggers the action.

➤ **Release**—The action doesn't happen until someone clicks on the button and releases the mouse button.

➤ **Release Outside**—The action only happens if a visitor clicks on the mouse, and then moves his or her cursor outside the Hit frame area of a button.

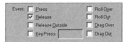

Figure 13.4

Theoretically, you could assign more than one mouse event to a button— but that is usually going to be either redundant or confusing. Best to pick one event to associate with a button. Here, Release is selected, meaning releasing the mouse button will trigger an action.

Nitty Gritty Stuff

What Triggers a Mouse Event?

Mouse events are trigger by a visitor clicking on the *hit* area of the mouse, which isn't necessarily the same as the visible button. The Hit frame area is the area defined by the shape you place in the Hit frame when you define (or edit) a button. For a full discussion of creating buttons and Hit frames, see Chapter 12, "Creating Control Buttons."

➤ **Roll Over**—This option activates a button action when a visitor hovers over the button without clicking.

➤ **Roll Out**—This option activates a button only after a visitor moves his or her mouse cursor over a button, and then off, without clicking.

➤ **Drag Over**—The action is activated only when a visitor clicks on the button, and then drags the mouse cursor off the button, and back on again.

➤ **Drag Out**—The action is activated when a visitor clicks on the button, and then drags the mouse cursor off the button.

Finally, you can also add a keystroke that will activate a button. For example, you might assign the End key on a keyboard to the last frame in a movie, or the Home key to the first frame.

Keep It Simple

Yes, technically there are seven different ways to define the mouse event that will activate a button. But since the goal is *usually* to make it *easy* for a visitor to activate a button, your real life choices basically boil down to Press—which activates the button when a visitor clicks on the button, Release—which is similar to Press except that the action is triggered by releasing the mouse button—or Roll Over, which activates the button when a visitor hovers over it.

One Button Per Keystroke

If you assign keystrokes to a button action, be careful to assign a unique keystroke to each button in a frame. Don't, for example, assign the right arrow key to two different buttons, or only one of them will actually be activated by the keystroke.

After you select an event, Flash will generate Action Script code on the right side of the box. Figure 13.5 shows this programming code in the Object Actions panel.

Figure 13.5

The On(Press) *code is generated by clicking on the Press check box on the right side of the dialog box. It just means "Do something when someone presses this button."*

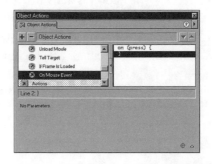

After you choose a triggering mouse event (like Press, or Roll Over), you can assign an action to a button.

Letting the Viewer Control the Action

One of the most basic ways to make a movie interactive is to allow a visitor to start and stop the movie. You can place buttons in frames that allow a viewer to do just that.

Figure 13.6 shows a frame with two buttons. The Stop this Movie Now and Start the Movie Again text has been added to the buttons to help the visitor figure out what to do.

Figure 13.6

One of the Flash clip art Button sets (in the Buttons Library) is a set of VCR-type controls. This is an intuitive way to help visitors stop, start, or fast-forward a movie.

After you place buttons on the page, use the five steps at the beginning of this chapter to begin defining the button action. Choose a mouse event to associate with the action, and then you can add stop and start actions to the button.

Hold That Pose!

To allow a visitor to stop a movie, assign the Stop action to the button:

1. Select the button and choose **Window**, **Actions** from the menu bar. This is a quick way to open the Object Actions panel for a selected button.
2. In the Object Actions panel, click on the + and choose Basic Actions from the flyout menu.
3. Click on OnMouseEvent and choose a mouse event (like Press).
4. With On(Press), or whatever mouse event you selected highlighted on the right side of the Object **Actions** panel, click on the + icon again, and choose Basic Actions, **Stop** from the list of actions in the pop-up menu. Your code will look like that in Figure 13.7.
5. Click **OK** to close the dialog box.

View or Hide Parameters

The Object Actions panel has two icons in the lower left corner of the panel. The Insert a Target path icon is used for more complex scripting than we're concerned with, but the other icon is handy. The Expand/Collapse the Parameters Area icon looks like a triangle, and toggles back and forth between displaying, or hiding script parameters. Because the On MouseEvent action has parameters (like Press, Roll Over, and so on), it's useful to display the parameters area when using that command. Other commands (like Stop) don't have parameters, and you can use the Expand/Collapse the Parameters Area icon to hide the parameters area when you don't need it.

Figure 13.7

The right side of the Object Actions panel lists the action that will be applied to the button. The Stop command is indented because it is part of a subprogram that begins by identifying a mouse event, and then tells Flash what to do when that mouse event happens. In this case, clicking on the mouse button will stop the movie.

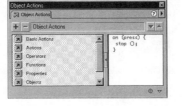

Of course, after you place a Stop button on a page, you'll probably want to add a button to restart the movie! To do that, follow the same steps, but change the command from Stop to Play.

Test your button by choosing **Control**, **Test Movie**, and clicking on your buttons in test mode to see how they work. Close the Test window to return to Flash's editing mode.

Adding Go To Actions to Jump To Frames

You can offer visitors the option of jumping to a frame in your movie. Visitors won't necessarily understand it's a *frame* that they are jumping to. You might want to offer them the option of jumping to the Feedback page, jumping to the Ordering page, or jumping to the Contact page.

If you're going to be setting up many of these Go To buttons, it will be helpful to label your frames. Do that by clicking on a Frame, and choosing **Modify**, **Frame** in the menu bar. In the **Label** area of the Frame panel, you can as-sign a name to your frame, as shown in Figure 13.8.

Backstage Pass

Making Actions Go Away

If you want to delete some code, just click on it and press the Delete key.

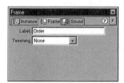

Figure 13.8

Labeling frames makes it easier to create buttons that jump to frames.

With your frames labeled, you can easily create buttons that link to frames with these steps:

1. Select the button and choose **Window**, **Actions** from the menu bar.

2. In the Object Actions panel, click on the + icon and select Basic Actions, On Mouse Event.

3. Choose a mouse event parameter (like On Press or On Release).

4. With the mouse event you selected high-lighted on the right side of the Object **Actions** panel, click on the + icon again, and choose Basic Actions, Go To from the list of actions in the pop-up menu.

5. If your movie has more than one scene, and you want to link the selected button to a frame in a different scene, choose that other scene from the Scene drop-down menu.

6. You can identify the target frame by number by entering a value in the Frame Number area. Or, you can choose Frame Label from

Backstage Pass

Making Actions Go Away

Scenes are a way of breaking up large movies into manageable "mini-movies." Scenes are discussed in Chapter 17, "Keeping It All Together."

the Type drop-down list, and enter the name of a labeled frame, as shown in Figure 13.9. Other options in the Type drop-down list.

Figure 13.9

You can program a button to jump to a named frame in a movie.

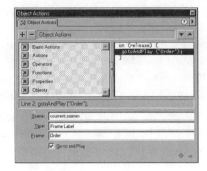

Go To and Play Versus Go To and Stop

The Go To action includes the Go To and Play parameter that is turned on or off using the check box in the Parameters area associated with this command. The default, Go To and Play (selected) jumps to a frame in a movie, and restarts the movie in that frame. If you deselect this option, the action jumps to the selected frame, but then stops the movie on that frame.

7. You can test your button by choosing **Control**, **Enable Simple Buttons**, and clicking on your buttons to see how they work. After testing your button, choose **Control**, **Enable Simple Buttons** again to toggle this feature off and once again edit buttons.

Adding Links to Web Sites

You can assign an action to a button that will open a Web page in the visitor's browser. To do this, select a button and choose **Window**, **Action**, and assign a mouse event to the button. Use the "+" flyout menu in the Action Options panel to choose Basic Actions, Get URL, and enter a Web address (a *URL*, or *uniform resource locator*) in the URL area of the Parameters area, as shown in Figure 13.10.

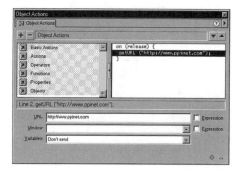

Figure 13.10

Buttons can be linked to Web addresses. Entering a URL in the URL area of the Get URL command generates the code Get URL ( )—*with the Web address you enter in the URL area inserted in the command.*

Nitty Gritty Stuff

Other Get URL Options

The Window drop-down list in the parameters area for the Get URL action allows you to define the target window for a link. Use this if you are creating a link from a framed page: _self opens the page in the current frame, _parent opens the page in the parent page of the open frame, and _top opens the page in the top-level frame of the current window. You can also use the _blank command to open the target page in a new browser window. The variables options are used if you are assigning buttons to scripts provided by a remote Web server.

To test a URL button, choose **File**, **Publish Preview**, **Default**. This opens your Flash movie in a Web browser. There, you can test your button. As soon as you move your cursor over a button with a URL link, the mouse cursor will change to a finger (in most browsers), as shown in Figure 13.11.

If you are connected to the Internet, you can test the link by activating the button—pressing it, rolling over it, or doing whatever mouse event you assigned to the button.

News Flash

Don't Forget http://

You must include http:// in the URL of the target Web site or your action will not jump the visitor to the desired site.

Figure 13.11

This button is linked to a Web site—you can tell because the browser displays a finger when the button is hovered over.

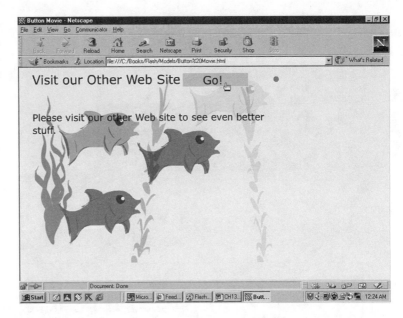

The Least You Need to Know

➤ Buttons can have actions attached to them.

➤ Every button with an action attached has to have a mouse event defined that will trigger the action. The most intuitive and user-friendly mouse events are Roll Over and Press.

➤ You can place a button on a frame to stop the movie, and to start it up again.

➤ Buttons can be used to allow a visitor to jump to a specific frame in a movie.

➤ Buttons can be used as links to Web pages.

Filling In the Blanks

In This Chapter

➤ Creating interactive movies

➤ Assigning stop actions to frames

➤ Collecting information in text fields

➤ Presenting input in a movie

A few years ago, some movie marketing genius came up the idea of letting the audience vote on how a movie would end. The idea was that people could see the "happy" or "sad" ending, and each time you went to the movie, you might see a different ending.

That marketing person was either ahead of his or her time, or wasting time, because customized movie endings didn't catch on. You can, however, create Flash movies that apply this concept. You can let viewers interact with your movie, allowing them to input information that is later used in the movie.

Interactive Movies

In Chapter 13, "Interacting with the Audience," you explored how Flash movies can include buttons that allow visitors to decide to stop a movie, to resume the movie, or to jump to a specific frame in a movie. That's one level of interactivity.

An even more interactive Flash movie will allow a visitor to enter text, and then use that text to customize the presentation. For example, in Figure 14.1, a Flash movie asked me my name, and then welcomed me to the presentation.

Figure 14.1

This Flash movie collected my name, and then displayed it. The data (my name) is stored in the movie for later use.

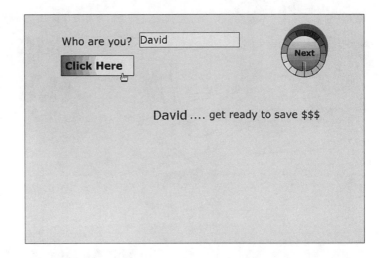

Later on in the movie, after more information has been collected, a frame displays both my name and the amount of money I might save, as shown in Figure 14.2.

Figure 14.2

You can collect multiple information fields, and combine the input results in a frame.

Data like the name and discount rate in Figure 14.2 is collected in *text fields*. These are special text boxes that collect data.

Before you can really collect data from visitors, you will want to stop the movie long enough for a visitor to do some typing. So, you'll start this chapter by adding Stop actions to frames, and then explore how to create text boxes that collect and display data.

Adding Stop Actions to Frames

The first thing you'll want to do when you collect data is to stop your movie. Stopping a movie freezes the presentation at the frame where you assign the Stop action. Normally movies that have a stop action associated with a frame also have a Play button, so visitors can resume the movie. Chapter 13 explains how to insert a Play button in a frame.

News Flash

Collecting Data in a Frame

Technically, you can create text boxes that create data without stopping a movie. But doing that can create some very hostile feelings among your visitors as they try to type in data before the movie continues. Better to stop the movie, let folks enter data, and then let them resume the movie with a Play button.

Actions and Frames

In Chapter 13, you examined how actions (like Stop or Play) can be associated with a button. When you click a button (or do some other defined event to a button—like roll over it—you can stop or start a movie.

You can also add actions like Stop to a movie frame independent of any button. These actions take effect when a frame displays without any action on the part of a visitor.

To add an action to a frame, make sure you do not have any objects selected, and choose Window, Actions. This will open the Frame Actions panel, as shown in Figure 14.3.

With the Frame Actions panel open, use the "+" flyout menu to add actions (like Stop) to a frame.

Figure 14.3

Many of the actions that can be assigned to frames involve rather complex programming. Others, like Stop or Stop All Sounds, are easy to use.

Actions and Layers

Every layer of every frame can have actions assigned to it. When you assign actions to more than one layer of a frame, the "chain of command" is that actions assigned to a higher layer happen before actions assigned to lower layers.

In real life, unless you are tweaking an unimaginably complex movie, you can assign all the actions you need to a single frame, and to keep things orderly, most Flash developers use the top level in a frame to store actions.

In Figure 14.4, for example, the top layer is called Actions, and is *just* used to store actions assigned to each frame.

Figure 14.4

In this movie, the top layer in each frame is used to hold actions, while the second layer holds the displayed objects.

Nitty Gritty Stuff

Complex Frame Actions

In this chapter, you'll look at the Stop action, and also how to use the Set Variable command to collect information from visitors that can be used in a movie. Other actions are beyond the scope of this book, but they include the Stop All Sounds action that turns off any sounds initiated in earlier frames (see Chapter 18, "Crank It Up!" for a full explanation of using sounds).

Adding a Stop Action to a Frame

Adding a Stop action to a frame brings your movie to a screeching halt at the frame to which the action is assigned.

One way to use the Stop action in a frame is when you don't want a movie to rerun after it's done playing. Or, you might have frames at the end of your movie that are only used as links to buttons (to link a button to a frame, see Chapter 13).

You can also use a Stop action along with a Play button in a frame. This way the movie will automatically stop until the visitor clicks the Play button to resume the action.

To assign a Stop action to a frame, follow these steps:

1. Select the frame and level to which you will add the Stop action.

2. Choose **Window**, **Actions**, to open the Frame Properties panel.

3. Click on the **+** icon and choose **Basic Actions**, **Stop** from the list of available actions.

4. You'll see a tiny "a" (for action!) in the Frame box in the Timeline.

After you assign a Stop action to a frame, you can test your movie by choosing **Control**, **Test Movie**.

Backstage Pass

Stop!

There are no parameters to set for the Stop action—it just stops the movie. After you click on the Stop action, "Stop" appears in the list of selected actions.

Creating Text Boxes

Text boxes collect text and/or values (numbers). This information can later be used in a movie to create an interactive experience for a visitor.

For example, you can find out a visitor's name, and then "talk to" your visitor by name later in the movie. Or, you can collect a value from a visitor (like how much he or she would like to invest in your new startup?), and your movie can "refer" to that value as shown in Figure 14.5.

Text boxes can be used for rather complex programming that's beyond the scope of this book, but with a minimum of programming (I promise!), we can use them to collect and then display information collected from visitors to create more interactive and personalized movies. In this section, I'll walk you through that process in detail, and along the way we'll check out how ActionScript is generated in Flash.

Figure 14.5

In this frame, the value entered into the text box with the line around it is collected as an input value. The Click Here button multiplies that value by 1.25, and the text box with the dotted line displays the resulting value.

To collect and display data, you need three things on a page:

➤ A **text field** that collects data and saves it as a variable.

➤ A **text field** that displays data collected in another text field.

➤ A **button** that will execute an action that displays data collected in one text field in another text field.

Collecting Data in a Text Field

Text fields are text boxes with a special property: they collect information from viewers during a movie. That information can then be "echoed" back during the movie to create a customized, personalized effect (As in, "Hi Janice...thanks for watching this video...").

To create a text field, first draw a regular text box with the text tool. Then, with the text box selected, choose Text, Options from the menu to open the Text Options panel, as shown in Figure 14.6.

Figure 14.6

The Text Options panel can be used to create input fields that collect data in a movie.

From the Text Type drop-down list in the Text Options panel, choose Input text.

In order to work, a text field must have a name. Flash will assign a name by default, but you can change that to a name you choose. To change the text field name, enter a new name in the Variable area of the Text Options panel.

The Text Options panel allows you to format the data you collect. The Line Type drop-down list lets you choose between a single line of input (for things like names, email addresses or zip codes), or multiline input for information that takes more than one line (like comments, feedback, or requests). The Password option in this drop-down lists displays input data as asterisks on the screen so it cannot be casually viewed by anyone watching the screen as it is typed in.

The Border/Bg check box displays the input field with a border. The Max Chars box allows you to restrict how many letters or numbers (or other characters) are typed into an input field.

The Embed fonts icons define how text will be displayed as it is entered in a field, and the HTML check box converts the input field to HTML code when the movie is published.

Backstage Pass

Leave Text Fields Blank

Don't enter any text in the text field. That's the job of viewers, who will type in text as they interact with your movie.

Backstage Pass

Easy to Remember Text Field Names

Later, you will need to use the text field name in an action. So, it's helpful to name a text field something easy to remember. For example, if you are collecting the name of a visitor, you could call the field Name.

Displaying Data in a Text Field

If you want to integrate collected data from a text field into a movie, you will need a second text field to *display* the collected data.

Create this text field by drawing a text box with the Text tool and activating the Text Options panel. Oddly enough, even though you are using this field to *display* collected information, you still want to use the Input Text option in the Text Type drop-down list.

Use the Variable box in the Text Options panel to enter a field name. Figure 14.7 shows a Text Field with a new name.

Figure 14.7

It can get confusing keeping track of which Text Field collects data, and which one displays that data. My trick is to name text fields that will display data as "outputfield1, outputfield2," and so on.

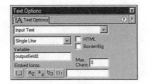

Rules for Text Field Variable Names

Text fields are also called *variables*. Text field (variable) names cannot contain spaces or symbols (like @, #, $, or *).

Creating a Button to Act on Collected Data

After you have defined a text field (a.k.a. a variable) to collect data, and a second text field to display that data, you can create a button that moves data from the input field into the output field when visitors view your movie.

To create this button, follow these steps:

1. You will need the (exact) names of the input text field (where you collect information), and the output text field (where you will display information). So it might be a good idea to write them on a piece of paper now.

2. Insert a button on your page.

Button, Button, Who's Got the Button?

Creating buttons is discussed in Chapter 12, "Creating Control Buttons." For a complete exploration of assigning actions to buttons, see Chapter 13.

3. With your button selected, choose **Window**, **Actions** to open the Object Actions panel. Choose Basic Actions, On MouseEvent from the + flyout menu. You can accept the default (on release) mouse event parameter, or click on another check box to change the mouse event that will trigger the action.

4. With the On(Release) line still selected, click the + icon again, and choose Actions, **Set Variable** from the flyout menu.

5. If the parameters area of the panel is not displayed, click the Expand/Collapse the Parameters Area icon in the lower right corner of the Object Actions panel to reveal the parameters area.

6. In the Variable box, enter the Variable name that you assigned to the text box that will *display* the collected data.

7. In the Value box, enter the Variable name you assigned to the text box that *collects* data.

8. Check the *second* Expression check box. Your dialog box should look something like the one shown in Figure 14.8, with your own Variable and Value names.

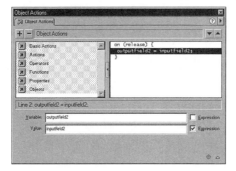

Figure 14.8

The Variable *is the name of the text box that displays* data, *the* Value *is the name of the text box that* collects *data. Highlight this in yellow in your book since nobody can remember which is which.*

Nitty Gritty Stuff

Express Yourself

Here's a brief explanation of the ActionScript we just generated:

We told Flash that our action would be triggered when someone clicked on a button, and that the action would be to convert the content of our output field into the content of our input field. The reason we checked the Expression check box for the Value field is so that Flash would know that we wanted the value of the variable in the text box inserted into the output field. If we didn't check the Expression check box, Flash would display the word "inputfield2" or whatever variable name we assigned instead of the value of the variable.

After you have defined the Variable and Value fields in the Object Actions panel, you can test your movie by choosing **Control**, **Test Movie**. Enter some text in your input box, click your button, and watch the text appear in the output box, as shown in Figure 14.9.

Figure 14.9

One text field collects data; the other displays it. The button activates the action that moves data from one to the other.

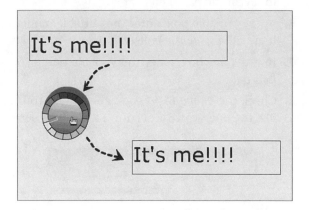

Creating a Button to Calculate Collected Data

One relatively simple thing you can do with collected data is to calculate it. For example, if you wanted to collect a visitor's age, you could display the year he was born by subtracting that value from the current year.

To apply a calculation to a Variable action, follow these steps:

1. Create two text fields, one that will collect a value, and another that will display a calculation based on that value.

2. Name the input field text field by selecting it, choosing Text, Options and entering a name in the Variable box.

3. Assign a Variable name to the output text field as well, and note both of your text field names.

4. Place a button on your page. With your button selected, choose **Window**, **Actions** to open the Object Actions panel.

5. In the Object Actions panel, choose Basic Actions, On MouseEvent from the + flyout menu.

6. With the On(Release)—or whatever mouse event you selected still highlighted, on the right side of the Object Actions panel, click the + icon again, and choose Actions, **Set Variable** from the list of actions.

7. Type the name of the text field *where the data will be displayed* in the Variable box. The Expression check box should be unchecked.

8. Type the name of the text field used to collect the data in the Value box. Check the Expression check box so that this information is treated as a field name, not as text.

9. You can add a calculation expression (+ to add, - to subtract, * to multiply, or / to divide) and another value. For example, to divide the value collected in the Variable box by 2, use **/2**, as shown in Figure 14.10.

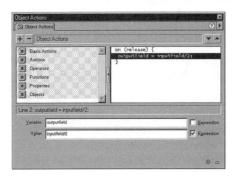

Figure 14.10

The action being assigned to the button will be divided by 2 and display the resulting value in the Text Field named output-field.

10. You can test your expression button by choosing **Control**, **Text Movie**.

Figure 14.11 shows two text fields, where a value entered into one field is divided by 2, and the result is displayed in the second field.

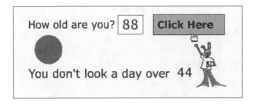

Figure 14.11

In this action frame, the top Text Field is the Value field, and is used to calculate the value that appears in the bottom Text Field, which is the Variable field.

Formatting Text Fields

Formatting text fields is similar to formatting text boxes except that there is no text. To define the font, size, and color of text in a text field, select a text field.

With the text field selected, use the Text menu to define Font, Font Size, or Font Style. Or, choose Text, Character from the menu to define Font Color, Bold or Italic attributes. Use the Text, Paragraph menu to define paragraph Alignment and spacing.

Backstage Pass

Formatting Text Fields

In this chapter, you've explored some fun ways to use variables to collect, display, and even calculate data. You'll look at how to use variables to further control your movie in Chapter 19, "Advanced Animation Techniques." Variables can also be used to create very complex movies that respond to all kinds of events.

If you're ready to immerse yourself in Flash ActionScript programming, pick up a copy of *Special Edition Using Flash 5* for a comprehensive exploration of ActionScript.

Outlines (or lack of them) around text fields are defined in the Text Options panel using the Border/Bg check box. Normally, if you are using a text field to *collect* data, you will want to display an outline around the field to make it obvious to a viewer where he or she should type text. You can, however, turn off the outline—this is especially effective when you are displaying *output* text, as shown in Figure 14.12.

Figure 14.12

The output text field has the outline turned off. The text is visible "through" the fish because the output text field is under the fish, and the fish is semi-transparent.

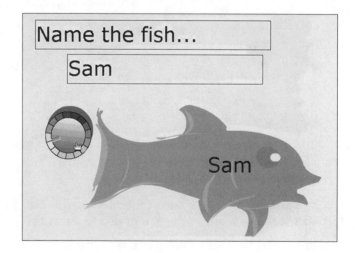

The Least You Need to Know

➤ Actions change the way a movie displays. Actions can be added to frames or to buttons.

➤ Frame actions must be assigned to a Layer, and often a separate (top) Layer is created to make it easy to keep track of actions.

➤ The Stop Action freezes a movie at the frame to which the action is assigned.

➤ Text fields can be used to collect or display data.

➤ Buttons can have actions assigned to them that collect data from one text field, and display it in another text field.

➤ Text fields can be formatted just like regular text boxes—except you assign font and paragraph attributes to the entire text box, not to any specific text.

Part 6
Animating with Flash Movies

Okay ladies and gentlemen, here's the moment you've been waiting for. In the following chapters, you'll learn to make those objects you've created hip, hop, and dance across the screen.

You'll learn to put together sequences of frames to create the appearance of movement in your movie. You'll learn to create animated scenes and organize those scenes into movies. And you'll explore Flash's "tween" feature that automates the process of creating animation.

Everybody Dance Now!

In This Chapter

➤ How Flash animates movies

➤ Creating keyframes

➤ Viewing multiple frames with Onion Skinning

➤ Testing animation

In Chapter 2, "Getting Around Backstage," we took a quick look at how to animate movies. It might seem like we've taken a long time to get back to animation. After all, isn't that what Flash is all about? Movies?

As you've seen in previous chapters, there is much more to Flash. You can create graphics objects, and save them as symbols—and use those symbols repeatedly (as instances). And you can create interactive buttons that react to visitor actions.

All of those features provide the building blocks for an animated Flash movie. And, as you'll see, in many ways animation is the *easy* part of working with Flash.

All that said, animation is the really fun and dynamic thing about Flash movies, so let's do it!

How Flash Animates

Flash creates animation by displaying multiple frames from a movie. In previous chapters we've pretty much restricted ourselves to creating images in a single frame. (The exception being the four-frame buttons we created in Chapter 12, "Creating Control Buttons.")

Flash creates two basic types of animation, tweened, and frame-by-frame animation. Tweened animation is automated animation, where you let Flash generate frames that create animation. We'll explore tweening in Chapter 16, "Automating Animation." In this chapter we'll look at frame-by-frame animation, where you define the contents of the frames.

When you create and manage animation in Flash, you focus much of your attention on the Timeline. The Timeline allows you to select different frames in a movie, and tells you the status of frames in a movie. Figure 15.1 displays some of the key elements of the Timeline.

Figure 15.1

Keyframes have defined content, while static frames in between them simply display the content of the last defined key frame.

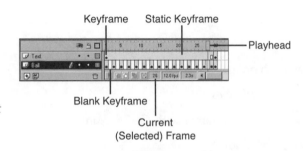

As you create frame-by-frame animation, you'll work with three kinds of frame content:

➤ **Keyframes** are frames where you insert content, like text and graphics.

➤ **Static Frames** are frames that don't have any content of their own, but continue to display the content of the preceding keyframe.

➤ **Blank Keyframes** are frames that don't display anything

Backstage Pass

Frames and Layers

Each layer has it's own set of definable frames. So, for example, Frame 30 in a movie could have a blank keyframe in one layer, a keyframe in another layer, and a static frame in a third layer, and so on.

Let's illustrate the three types of frames with a simple example. In Figure 15.2, The Text layer consists of two keyframes—one in frame 1, and one in frame 30. Each of these keyframes has the same content, (the company logo for ppinet.com), in the same location. The frames in between frame 1 and frame 30 in the Text layer are *Static* frames. They simply display the content of frame 1 all the way through the movie. In other words, the text just sits on the screen, in the same place, throughout the movie.

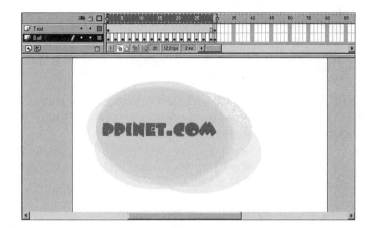

Figure 15.2

This movie combines keyframes, static frames, and blank keyframes to project static text, while shapes strobe on and off in different locations in the background.

The Ball layer in the movie has many keyframes. By turning on Onion Skinning we can see that the ball moves around during the movie. Each of the sixteen keyframes in the Ball layer has unique, distinct content—namely the oval ball—in a different location.

Finally, the Ball layer also contains 14 *blank* keyframes. These are frames with no content. When the movie projects these frames, no content will be projected from the Ball layer, although the static frames in the Text layer will continue to display text throughout the movie.

The effect of combining keyframe, static frames, and blank frames is that the text appears on the screen, while ovals appear and disappear in different locations behind the text.

Backstage Pass

Blank Keyframes

Onion Skinning reveals the content of many frames at once. We'll explore this in detail in the section "Viewing Multiple Frames with Onion Skinning," later in this chapter.

Inserting Keyframes

Inserting a keyframe creates a new keyframe with the *same contents* as the selected keyframe. You *automatically* create a keyframe in frame one when you add content to the frame (try it: create a new movie, and add content to the first frame. You'll see a small black circle appear in the Timeline indicating that the first frame is a keyframe).

With one keyframe created, you can generate new, identical keyframes by clicking on a frame in the Timeline, and choosing Insert, Keyframe from the menu. As you do, the contents of the previous keyframe will be placed in your new keyframe.

Creating Frame-by-Frame Motion with Keyframes

Keyframes allow you to *change* the location of objects. After you generate a new keyframe, Flash will duplicate the objects in the selected keyframe, but now you can move the objects around.

If all you do is leave the generated copy of your object(s) in the original location, there will not be any motion in your movie. But if you move the object in the new keyframe, the object will appear to move when the movie is viewed.

Backstage Pass

Blank Keyframes

In addition to the menu option for inserting a keyframe, there is an option for inserting a blank keyframe. Inserting a blank keyframe creates a new keyframe, but you have to create new objects in it from scratch. The contents of the previous keyframe will not be inserted into a blank keyframe.

Generating Static Frames

Often, animated movies include layers that have motion, and layers that have objects that just "sit there" in one place.

To create a layer with content that says in one place throughout the movie, first create the content of the static layer in Frame 1. Then, click in what will be the final frame of the movie, and **Insert**, **Keyframe**, as shown in Figure 15.3. The content of Frame 1 will be duplicated.

Figure 15.3

The keyframe being created in Frame 20 will duplicate the content of the keyframe in Frame 1. All the frames in between will have generated static content that continues to display the content of frame 1 all the way to Frame 20.

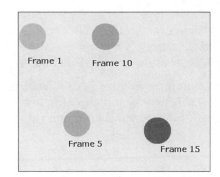

Creating Blank Keyframes

What if, for some reason, you don't want a shape in Frame 1 to be duplicated for all the frames in your movie? For example, you might want a shape (or text) to appear in *some frames*, and then later disappear.

To convert a frame to a *blank* frame, you must convert it to what Flash calls a *blank keyframe*. Turn a static frame into a blank keyframe by selecting the frame, and choosing **Insert**, **Blank Keyframe**.

Keyframes Move

You can click and drag on a keyframe, and move it around on the Timeline.

Inserting a blank keyframe *ends* the static display of the previous keyframe. A white rectangle will appear in the frame before the blank keyframe that displays the tooltip "Static." This marks the end of the static display, as shown in Figure 15.4.

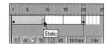

Figure 15.4

The Static icon in the Timeline marks the end of the display of the content of the previous keyframe.

Putting It All Together

To help grasp how keyframes, blank keyframes, and static frames work together in animation, try this little example:

1. Create a new Flash movie with three layers (from top to bottom): Text, Spotlight, and Background, as shown in Figure 15.5.

Figure 15.5

The Text layer will have animated objects using frame-by-frame animation. The Background layer will have a static image. And the Spotlight layer will use keyframes and blank keyframes to "turn a light on."

2. In frame one of the Text layer, enter some text in the upper right corner of the stage.

3. Click in the Text layer of the Timeline to select Frame 5, and press the F6 function key to create a new keyframe. The text is duplicated in Frame 5. Click and drag to move the text halfway down the stage.

4. Click in Frame 10, and choose **Insert**, **Keyfram**e again to create a new keyframe. Drag the text to the lower right corner of the stage.

5. Click in Frame 20, and choose **Insert**, **Keyframe** again to generate the final keyframe. Don't move the text this time—the movie will display the text in the same location from Frames 10–20. At this point, your movie should look something like the one in Figure 15.6.

Figure 15.6

The Text layer has four keyframes. These keyframes provide marking points for the motion the text will go through as the movie is played.

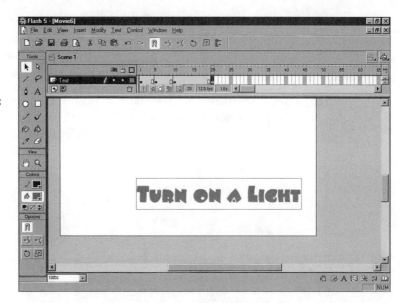

6. To create the static background for the movie, select the first frame of the Background layer, and draw a gray rectangle that fills most of the stage. Then click in the 20th frame of the Background layer, and press the F6 function key to create a new keyframe. As you do, Flash automatically generates static frames in the Background layer that fill the rest of the movie, as shown in Figure 15.7.

Figure 15.7

When you add a keyframe to a layer, Flash automatically generates static frames that display the content of the keyframe.

7. Finally, we'll use the spotlight layer to create a yellow "light" that "turns on" in Frame 15. To do this, click in Frame 15 in the Spotlight layer, and press the **F6** function key. A new blank keyframe is created in Frame 15 of the Spotlight layer, but the previous frames are *blank keyframes*.

8. Draw a yellow circle in the Spotlight layer of Frame 15. Then click in the Spotlight layer of Frame 20, and choose **Insert**, **Keyframe** to create a new keyframe. The "spotlight" will display in Frames 15-20, but the Spotlight layer will have nothing but blank frames for the first 14 frames of the movie.

9. Finally, you can watch your movie in Flash by choosing **Control**, **Rewind** (to rewind the movie to Frame 1), and then choosing Control, Play.

Backstage Pass

Faster Controls

For faster and easier control over rewinding and playing movies, see the section "Using the Control Window," a bit later in this chapter.

In this little exercise you to created and played a movie using keyframes, static frames, and blank frames. Before we move onto more complex animation (in the next chapter), we'll examine how to view animation in Flash.

Viewing Animation

Flash animations are ultimately saved in Flash's *.fla movie format, where they can be seen using the Flash movie viewer. This viewer is embedded in Microsoft Internet Explorer 5 and higher, and is available as a plug-in for Netscape Navigator. In Chapter 21, "Putting Flash Online," you'll explore that process in detail.

Alternatively, you can export Flash movies to a variety of formats including animated GIF files and AVI video files. Export options are explained in Chapter 22, "Exporting Flash Movies."

You can, however, check out and test your animation before you publish your movie as a Flash movie file or export it to another animation format. In Flash itself, you can use Onion Skinning to see multiple frames at once, and you can use the Control window to run your movie right in Flash.

Viewing Multiple Frames with Onion Skinning

Turn on Onion Skinning by clicking the Onion Skin or Onion Skin Outlines icons under the Timeline (see Figure 15.9). Even without running a movie, you can view many frames at once using Onion Skinning. To do this, click and drag in the frames in the **Timeline**, and click the **Onion Skin** icon below the Timeline, as shown in Figure 15.8.

Timeline Header

Figure 15.8

Here, onion skinning is applied only to Frames 5 through 10. Click and drag in the Timeline Header to define which frames are displayed.

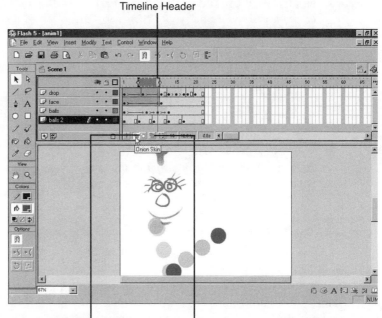

Onion Skin Outlines   Edit Multiple Frames

The Onion Skin Outlines icon changes the objects displayed by onion skinning to outlines—which can be helpful with a cluttered movie full of busy frames.

You can also edit multiple frames at once by selecting the Edit Multiple Frames icon. This gives you the power to edit all selected frames at once.

News Flash

Don't Forget What Frame You're In

The downside of editing all frames at once is that it's easy to mess up your anima-tion by moving an object without realizing what frame it is in. Generally speaking you will want to invoke this option only occasionally, for the specific purpose of moving objects in frames *in relation to each other*. Then return to single frame editing for most of your work.

Using the Control Window

To actually *play* your movie without leaving Flash, just choose **Control**, **Play** (or press (Return) [Enter] on your keyboard). For more control, you can use the Play (and other) controls in the Control window. View this window by choosing **Window**, **Toolbars**, **Controller**.

The Controller keys look intuitively like many online video player controls. Figure 15.9 identifies each button in the Control window.

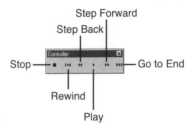

Figure 15.9

The handy Control window can be dragged around the screen by clicking and dragging on the title bar. It can be docked into the standard toolbar by dragging it to the right side of that toolbar.

To test a movie, click the Rewind button first (to start from Frame 1), and then click the Play button to see your video in action.

You can step through a movie frame-by-frame by using the Step Forward button.

Testing Movies in the Flash Viewer

In addition to running your movie in Flash, you can see how your movie will look in the Flash Viewer. Do this by choosing **Control**, **Test Movie** from the menu.

After you've tested your movie in the Flash Viewer, click on the Close button in the Viewer to return to Flash.

Testing Movies in the Flash Viewer

In order to test a movie in the Flash Viewer, Flash creates a temporary *.swf file. If you opened a file from a folder or device (like a CD) that does not allow you to save files to it, you will need to first save your movie to another folder before you can test it in the Flash viewer.

Backstage Pass

Other Movie Properties

The Movie Properties dialog box also allows you to change the background color, and change the size of the "movie screen."

Changing Frame Rate

The Movie Properties dialog box (choose **Modify**, **Movie**) allows you to control animation and other elements that apply to your entire movie. Here, you can speed up or slow down your movie.

The Frame Rate box in the Movie Properties dialog box determines how fast your movie plays. Faster frame rates create smoother movies. A very slow frame rate, like .5 frames per second (FPS for short) will present your movie almost like a slide show instead of an animated movie.

Further complicating all this is that frame rate is affected by how the speed of a viewer's computer processor. If a Flash movie is displayed on an old 486 at 30 fps, it will slow way down because the computer can't handle that kind of frame rate. Twelve frames per second is the generally accepted standard for Flash movies.

The Least You Need to Know

➤ Animation is created by placing objects in more than one frame.

➤ Adding keyframes creates new frames with the content of the selected frame. That content can be moved to create the sensation of motion when the movie is viewed.

➤ You can test a movie in Flash by opening the Controller window and using the Rewind and Play buttons to view the movie.

➤ The speed of a movie is determined by the frame per second rate—defined in the Movie Properties dialog box.

LET'S MOVE IT PEOPLE!!

Automating Animation

In This Chapter

➤ Creating flowing animation with tweening

➤ Defining animation paths with motion lines

➤ Rotating and resizing tweened animation

➤ Morphing shapes with animation

➤ Using animated masks

In Chapter 15, "Everybody Dance Now!" you looked at frame-by-frame animation. You moved objects from frame to frame, but the motion was sudden, jerky, and abrupt.

By changing the transitions between frames to more gradual and gradated motion, your movie can depict moving characters, flowing motion, and really start to look like...a *movie*!

There are two ways to do this:

You could painstakingly create thousands of frames by hand, adding minute alterations to each frame so that when shown together, they created the perception of natural, flowing motion.

Or...you can let Flash do that work. If you're inclined to turn that tedious task over to Flash, you're reading the right book!

Symbols and Tweening

The process of creating many sequential frames that merge the motion between other frames is called tweening, from the fact that this process creates frames in between other frames. *Keyframes* are the "decision points" in your animation. They define nodal points in an animated sequence, and Flash generates motion between them. Anywhere where you want to control the action is where you will put a keyframe.

Tweening is most often used to create smooth motion between frames, but it can also be used to gradually morph one shape into another. You'll explore both kinds of tweening in this chapter.

Creating Tween Frames

Tweening is easy. Setting up your movie so that you're ready to apply tweening is the difficult part. But if you're comfortable with the basic concepts of symbols, layers, and animation that we've covered in previous chapters, tweening is a breeze.

To create a tween frame, you must start with at least two keyframes. Because you will usually want to define tweening for specific objects within a movie, it is important to place each object in its own layer (see Chapter 8, "Working with Layers," for a full explanation of how to do that).

Tweening can only be applied to instances of symbol objects. So, if you're a bit hazy on Symbols, it will be helpful to review the discussion of Symbols and instances in Chapter 10, "Recycling with Symbols."

Adding Tweening

To apply tweening, first click and drag to select the leftmost of two keyframes in a layer, or the frames in between them. Then, with the frames selected, choose **Insert**, **Create Motion Tween** from the menu, as shown in Figure 16.1.

In Figure 16.2, I've left on Onion Skinning to display the additional frames generated by applying Motion Tween between the keyframes in the layer.

Symbols and Tweening

Flash generates tween motion by altering instances of Symbols. If you try to generate tween motion between cells with graphics objects that are not Symbols, Flash will let you get away with that. But, behind the scenes, Flash will generate Symbols for you, and assign them names like Tween1, Tween2, Tween3, and so on. In order to control the process, and keep track of your symbols, you're better off converting your graphics objects into Symbols yourself.

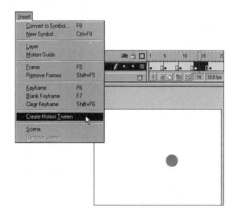

Figure 16.1

Motion tween will generate smooth motion in the section of frames selected in the Timeline.

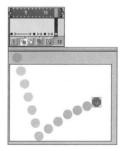

Figure 16.2

Onion skinning reveals the effect of adding tween frames between keyframes.

Creating a Motion Guide

A *motion guide* is an invisible line that you can use to define a motion path between tweened keyframes. For example, a falling leaf can follow a circuitous route from a tree to the ground—defined by a line you draw with the pencil tool.

To create a motion guide, select the frames between tweened keyframes, and choose **Insert**, **Motion Guide** from the menu, as shown in Figure 16.3.

Figure 16.3

The current motion of the ball, as shown through onion skinning, is a straight diagonal line. That can be altered with a motion guide.

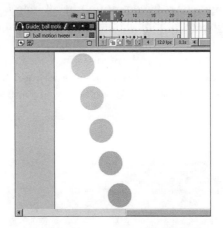

When you insert a motion guide, a new layer appears above your selected layer, with a layer name that starts "Guide:..." followed by the name of the layer to which the guide will be applied.

In the Guide layer, you can use the Pencil (or Pen, or Straight Line) tool to draw a path for the tweened object to follow, as shown in Figure 16.4.

Figure 16.4

The motion guide path defines a curve in the line of the ball as it falls.

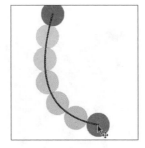

You can test tweened movie by choosing **Control, Rewind**, and then **Control, Play** from the menu. The motion line will *not* be visible when your movie is viewed in the Flash viewer.

Nitty Gritty Stuff

Objects Must Be Near the Motion Path

If you draw the motion path line so that the start is too far away from the object start, or the end is too far away from the object end, then the tweening will not follow the motion path until you move the start and/or finish objects closer to the path.

Adding Rotation and Scaling to a Tween

In addition to defining a motion guide for tweened frames, you can also add rotation to a symbol as it moves through the tween process.

To add rotation to the path of a tweened animation, rotate the symbol instance in one of the keyframes, as shown in Figure 16.5.

Figure 16.5

Rotating an object in the second keyframe in the series of tweened frames will add incremental rotation to the face in each frame.

More Fun Tweening Techniques

You can change the Alpha (transparency) of Symbol instances to create the effect of objects "fading in" or out as they move through an animation sequence. Alter the Alpha setting for a symbol instance by selecting the instance in a keyframe and choosing **Window, Panels, Effect**.

To alter the transparency of an instance of a symbol, choose Alpha from the drop-down list in the Effect panel, and assign a percentage of less than 100% to add some transparency, as shown in Figure 16.6. Lower Alpha percentages equal more transparency.

Figure 16.6

Alpha settings define opacity—which is the opposite of transparency. So, high Alpha settings provide little transparency, while low settings create very transparent objects.

Another fun technique is to create the illusion of an object coming towards the viewer by increasing the size of the final keyframe in a tweened animation sequence.

In Figure 16.7, the red ball changes from small to large, and from semi-transparent to fully opaque as it twirls through the air and falls toward the viewer.

Figure 16.7

This tweened animation sequence is shown here with onion skinning, revealing the ball getting larger as it falls toward the bottom of the stage.

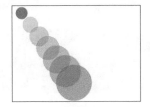

Changing Tweening for Selected Frames

If you click on a tweening arrow in frames, the tweening setting Frame panel will affect all the tweening indicated by the arrow.

Removing Tweening

Tween motion is displayed in the timeline as blue shading between frames, with an arrow running between keyframes. When it becomes necessary to remove tweening from an animation, click on the blue shading in any of the tweened frames and choose **Modify**, **Frames** to open the Frame panel.

From the Tweening drop-down list, choose **None**, as shown in Figure 16.8. This removes tweening motion from all frames in the tweened sequence.

Figure 16.8

Tweening can be removed in the Frame Properties dialog box.

Shape Tweening

In addition to tweening changes in the *location* of symbol instances, you can also tween changes in the *shape* of symbol instances.

Shape tweening gracefully morphs between two shapes to produce some really cool effects, including facial changes in a character, as shown in Figure 16.9.

Figure 16.9

Onion skinning reveals the "two faces" that will be morphed into each other through shape tweening. The frown face will morph into a smile.

Using Drawings for Shape Tweening

Unlike motion tweening, you *can't* use symbols to create shape tweening. Instead, you can just create two drawings in different keyframes, and apply shape tweening to morph from one to the other.

An Easy Shape Tween

The following quick, simple exercise will demonstrate how shape tweening works:

1. In a new movie, use the Pencil tool to draw a face in Frame 1 with a frown.

2. Create a new keyframe in Frame 10. The face will be duplicated in the new keyframe.

3. Delete the frown mouth from the duplicated keyframe, and draw a new smile mouth using the Pencil tool.

4. Click in the Timeline on a frame between Frame 1 and Frame 9 to select all 9 frames.

5. With the frames selected, choose Modify Frame to open the Frame panel, and choose **Shape** from the Tweening drop-down list in the **Tweening** tab, as shown in Figure 16.10.

199

No Symbols Allowed

Not only can you not use symbols in shape tweening, you cannot use grouped objects either. That's because shape tweening morphs (changes) *each element* of a graphic and needs to identify what these objects are. If you try to apply shape tweening to grouped objects, you'll see a friendly warning from Flash that this won't work.

Another visual aid that indicates a problem with either a motion tween or shape tween is the 'dotted' arrow between the keyframes. When you see a dotted arrow, that means Flash trying to generate tweening, but there is a problem with how you have asked Flash to do this.

Figure 16.10

As soon as you select Shape in the Tweening drop list in the Frame panel, an arrow and green shading in the Timeline indicate that you have successfully generated a shape tween.

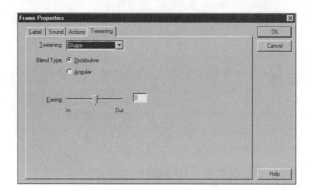

   6. Test your shape tween by using the Controller window to play your movie.

Animating with Masking

Imagine yourself traveling on an ocean liner looking out one of those little porthole windows at the ocean. A mask layer in a Flash movie works like the window on the ocean liner. It provides a "window" to view other layers.

Masking requires at least two layers: the mask layer, and at least one layer under the mask. You can animate the mask, and any or all of the layers under the mask.

Shape Tweening Options

When you choose **Shape** from the **Tweening** drop-down menu in the Frame panel, you can use the Blend drop-down list and the Easing slider to control how shapes are transformed. Distributive Blend Type blends shapes more smoothly, while Angular retains angles as shapes change. A high Easing value increases the speed of the transition at the beginning of a morph, and a low Easing value speeds up the changes at the end of the transition. An Easing setting of zero maintains an even pace of tweening between shapes.

Creating a Masking Layer for a Movie

If you have an existing movie, you can place a mask layer over it. Do that by first inserting a layer, and moving the new layer to the top of your layers.

To turn a selected layer into a mask, choose **Modify**, **Layer**, and click on **Mask** in the Layer Properties dialog box, as shown in Figure 16.11.

As soon as you click **OK** on the Layer Properties dialog box, the selected layer appears with a down arrow next to it.

Keeping Layers Straight

To keep yourself organized, it's handy to name the mask layer Mask.

Figure 16.11

Turning a layer into a mask. To keep life from getting too confusing, I've named the layer "Mask" as well as assigning mask properties to it.

201

Assigning Masked Properties Layers

The next step is to assign Masked layer status to those layers that you want to be covered up by the mask (and exposed by any shapes in the mask).

Assign masked status to layers by selecting a layer and choosing **Modify**, **Layer** from the menu. Click the **Masked** options button, and then click **OK**. Figure 16.12 shows a movie with four masked layers under a mask layer.

Figure 16.12

The masked layers will appear to be "under" the mask layer, and will only be visible when a shape in the mask layer is on top of them.

After you've defined both a mask and one or more masked layers, the next step is to create objects on the mask layer that will serve as lenses into the masked layers below. A simple form of a mask is to just create an animated circle, like the one in Figure 16.13.

Figure 16.13

The circle is on the mask layer. The monkey and the rest of the scenery are on masked layers underneath. Note that all layers are locked, allowing the mask to display as it will in a movie.

In order to test your mask, you need to lock all layers and play the animation using the Controller window. You can adjust the mask location by unlocking layers and moving the mask.

The Least You Need to Know

➤ Tweening "fills in" frames in between keyframes with smoothly animated frames.

➤ Only symbols can be tweened.

➤ Special layers can be created to hold motion lines that define an animation.

➤ Shapes can also be tweened so that they seamlessly morph from one shape to another.

➤ Masking is a technique for creating an overlay layer that serves as a lens to look at other layers.

LET'S HAVE THE MOUSE HIT THE CAT WITH A SACK OF MACKERELS!!

GOTCHA!

Keeping It All Together

In This Chapter

➤ Creating animated symbols

➤ Creating movie clips

➤ Plugging animated symbols and movie clips into movies

➤ Organizing movies into scenes

As developers use Flash to create wholly animated worlds on Web sites, movies can have hundreds of layers and thousands of frames.

There are a couple of different techniques for keeping big movies manageable as you edit them. One is to utilize animated symbols. *Animated symbols* are like static (non-animated) symbols except that they have action. So, in that sense, an animated symbol is actually a little movie in its own right. By plugging animated symbols into movies, you can keep your Timeline relatively clear while generating a lot of action on screen.

Nitty Gritty Stuff

Animated Symbols?

There are three *basic* types of symbols in Flash: Movie Clips, Buttons, and Graphics. You save file size by converting drawings into symbols and reusing them in a movie. Chapter 10, "Recycling with Symbols," breaks down how graphic symbols are created and used, focusing on static graphic symbols. Button symbols are four-frame symbols that define the up, over, and down states for a button. See Chapter 12, "Creating Control Buttons," for a full explanation of button symbols. In this chapter, we're focusing on a third type of symbol—Movie Clips.

So where do animated symbols fit in? Graphic symbols *can be animated*. How? When you edit a symbol, you can use *more than one frame*, and you can use all the tweening options you can use in a movie (like motion tweening).

Unlike other symbols, animated symbols continue to "play" beyond the frame they are embedded in. So, for example, if an animated symbol has 40 frames and is placed in the first frame of a movie, it will continue to play until frame 40, even though it will appear in the Timeline only in Frame 1.

Backstage Pass

Using Shape-Tweened Animations as Symbols

Because they don't "move" around the screen, shape tweens are especially handy when saved as animated graphics symbols. Twinkling stars, flashing lights, blinking logos, and rotating icons can be converted to animated symbols, and conveniently inserted into movies as symbols.

Movie clips are a little different than animated graphics symbols—mainly in that they play continuously throughout a movie while animated graphics symbols play only once.

For more complex movies, movie scenes can be cut out of long movies and pasted together. Organizing movies into scenes is even more useful when combined with frame actions and button actions that allow visitors to jump from one section of a movie to another. In this chapter, I'll walk you through the process of cutting up a movie into bite-sized scenes.

Backstage Pass

Sometimes Animated Symbols Loop

If you drop an animated graphic symbol onto the stage and give it more frames in the Timeline than in the animated graphic symbol, the animated symbol will loop.

Creating Animated Symbols

There are two ways to create an animated symbol. You can convert an existing animation (or part of it) to an animated symbol, or you can create an animated symbol from scratch.

Which to use? Depends on what you're starting from. If you are creating an animated clip specifically to use as a symbol, you can easily create the movie in the Symbol window.

If you already have an animation, you can wrap up and package that animated sequence as an animated symbol.

Backstage Pass

Three Ways to Organize Animated Clips

Because the process of creating an animated graphics symbol is very similar to creating a movie clip or a movie scene, we will walk through the process in detail. Later, I'll discuss how the process differs a bit for movie clips and scenes.

Creating an Animated Symbol from Scratch

Creating an animated symbol is very much like creating a movie, only you do it in Symbol window. Here's how:

1. Choose **Insert**, **New Symbol** from the menu.
2. Enter a symbol name in the Name box of the Symbol Properties dialog box, and choose the **Graphic** option button. Click **OK**. You can tell you are in the Symbol window because the name of the symbol appears above the Timeline, along with a link to the scene (movie) you are editing, as shown in Figure 17.1.
3. Create your animated symbol just as you would a movie. When you finish, click on the Scene link to save your animated symbol to your movie library.

Link to Movie

Figure 17.1

Editing a symbol is similar to editing a movie—including in that you can use multiple frames to create animation in a symbol.

After you click on the Scene link above the Timeline to return to the movie window, your new animated symbol will appear in your Symbol Library (choose **Window, Library** from the menu).

Animated symbols are displayed in the preview area of the Symbol Library window with a small play button in the upper-right corner of the window. Click that button, as shown in Figure 17.2, to preview the animated symbol.

Figure 17.2

The Play button in the Library window previews animated symbols. It is only active when a symbol is animated.

Converting Animated Layers into an Animated Symbol

A movie, or a section of a movie, can be converted into an animated symbol. Later, that animated symbol can be plugged into a larger movie.

Embedding Symbols in Symbols

When you create animated symbols, you can save time and file size by embedding *other* already existing symbols.

To transform a section of a movie into an animated symbol, first click and drag to select all the frames and layers of the movie that you want to convert into an animated symbol. Choose **Edit, Copy Frames**.

After copying frames to the clipboard, choose **Insert, New Symbol**. Enter a name for the symbol, and choose the **Graphic** option button. Click **OK**, and then click in the first frame of the new symbol window. With the frame selected, choose **Edit, Paste Frames** (make sure to select Paste *Frames*). Your animation has now been converted into a symbol.

Using Animated Symbols in Movies

Plugging animated symbols into movies can be a little confusing because they appear to reside in just one frame. An animated symbol is actually its own little (or not so little) movie, with many frames. And it will run until it has displayed all its frames.

In order for all the frames in an animated symbol to display in the movie, the layer in which the animated symbol is placed must have enough frames to display all the frames in the symbol. So, for example, if you are embedding an animated symbol with 10 frames in a layer, that layer's Timeline must have at least 10 frames. If there are additional frames, the animated symbol will repeat.

Creating Movie Clips

Movie clips are created exactly the same way as animated graphic symbols, except that you choose Movie Clip in the Symbol Properties dialog box, instead of Graphic.

Movie clips display in the Symbol Library with a distinctive icon next to them—you can see that icon in Figure 17.3.

Backstage Pass

Copy Frames!

Be sure to choose **Edit**, **Copy Frames** instead of just **Edit**, **Copy**. Only Copy *Frames* will place copies of all your frames in the clipboard for pasting in the symbol window.

Backstage Pass

Adding Frames—An Example

If your animated graphic symbol has 20 frames, and you paste it in the first frame of a one-frame movie, you will need to extend the layer in which the graphic is placed by 19 more frames. A quick, easy way to do this is to click in Frame 20 and press the F6 function key (the shortcut for **Insert**, **Keyframe**).

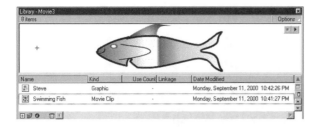

Figure 17.3

Movie clips appear in the Library with a distinctive icon, and in Wide View, the Library lists Movie Clip in the Kind column.

You can take a look at the template movie clips that come with Flash by choosing **Windows**, **Common Libraries**, **Movie Clips** from the menu. It might be helpful to drag a movie clip from that library onto the stage to experiment with as you read this section of this chapter.

Backstage Pass

Movie Clips and Actions

One of the biggest differences between movie clips and animated graphic symbols is the ability to control the movie clip using actions. You can setup a button, for example, to start and stop a movie clip. Adding actions to buttons is explored in Chapter 13, "Interacting with the Audience."

Both movie clips and graphic symbols are created by using multiple frames in the New Symbol library. Both animated graphics symbols and movie clips are placed in a single frame in a movie. So, what's the difference?

Movie clips are more "independent" than animated graphics symbols. You cannot view the animation from a movie clip in Flash edit mode using the Control window. You must use **Control**, **Test Movie** to view a movie clip in action. And, movie clips do not have to be placed in a layer that has enough frames to display all the frames in the movie clip.

You can place a movie clip in a single frame layer, and the whole movie clip will still display.

Figure 17.4 shows an instance of a movie clip symbol placed in a single frame of a layer.

Figure 17.4

A movie clip symbol is independent of other frames in a layer. It runs until it is done, even if it goes beyond other action in the layer. Animated and movie clips are best previewed by choosing ***Control***, ***Test Movie***.

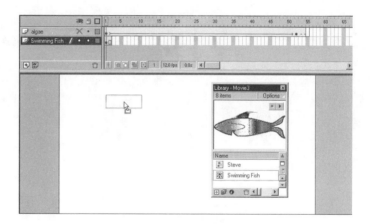

Backstage Pass

When to Use Which?

If you want an animated sequence to play *once* during a movie, you're likely best off with an animated graphics symbol. Set the instance to play only once. If you want an animation that *repeats throughout a movie*, go with a movie clip symbol.

Creating a Scene

Animated graphics symbols and movie clip symbols are good ways to store chunks of a movie in an easy-to-manage place. Because graphics symbols and movie clip symbols can have hundreds of frames in them, you can produce quite a complex animation by integrating these animated symbols into your Flash movie.

Scenes are an additional way to manage large movies. But scenes are really not much different than movies, except that they play in sequence. Think of scenes as similar to the reels of a movie shown in a theater—when one reel ends, the next one starts (if the projectionist hasn't dozed off!). Scenes are a way to keep very large movies in manageable pieces when you edit them.

There are two negatives to scenes. One is that they can make your movie more unwieldy and confusing to keep track of. The other is that when you present a movie, the process of downloading each scene from a server can disrupt the flow of the movie. For these reasons, scenes are only advisable for very large and complex movies, and kind of press up against the limits of our "for complete idiots" format.

However, you may find scenes useful if your movie is hundreds of frames long, or if you will be using actions to allow visitors to view different sections of your movie. Applying actions is covered in Chapter 19, "Advanced Animation Techniques."

Breaking Movies into Scenes

You can create and manage scenes using the Scene Inspector. To open that inspector, choose **Window**, **Panels**, **Scene**. By default, your movie will have just one scene, as shown in Figure 17.5.

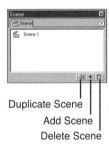

Duplicate Scene
Add Scene
Delete Scene

Figure 17.5

By default, every movie starts with one scene, called—creatively enough—Scene 1.

You can add additional scenes by clicking on the **Add** button, and delete a selected scene by clicking on the **Delete** button.

The **Duplicate** button creates, as you might expect, a duplicate of the selected scene. This can be handy when you want to create a slightly altered version of your selected scene. You might use an altered copy of a scene in a scenario where you are repeating a presentation, and want to vary it a bit.

You can use the Scene panel to move between scenes in your movie. Just to keep you from getting too confused, Flash displays the active scene just above the Timeline in the Edit window.

After you add a new scene, you can copy and paste frames into that new scene from other scenes. Use the **Copy Frames** and **Paste Frames** options from the **Edit** menu to copy and paste frames from one scene to another, and use the Scene Panel to toggle from one scene to another.

Combining Scenes into Movies

When you test a movie (choose **Control**, **Test Movie**), you will see all the scenes in your movie run sequentially, in the order they are listed in the Scene panel.

If you want to reorder scenes in your movie, you can click and drag on scenes in the Scene panel, as shown in Figure 17.6.

Figure 17.6

You can edit a movie by juggling the order in which scenes are presented. Here, a scene with introductory music is being moved to the beginning of the movie.

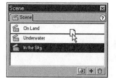

The Least You Need to Know

➤ Animated graphics symbols and movie clips are two similar ways to store mini-movies as symbols.

➤ Animated graphics symbols and movie clip symbols can both be placed in a movie frame.

➤ Animated graphics symbols require enough frames to display all the frames in the symbol, and can be set to play only once, while movie clip symbols play repeatedly as long as a movie plays.

➤ Very large movies can be broken into scenes.

➤ Scenes can be reordered to change the way a movie is presented.

Crank It Up!

Before the Advent of Flash (referred to in Biblical terms as BF), sound files in Web sites tended to be annoying. Not because there was anything inherently annoying about the content of them (although some of the pulsing synthesized beats got a little maddening). But because there was very little a Web developer or a Web visitor could do to control the sound. No way to turn it on, turn it off, or change it, without lunging for the volume control on his system.

Flash provides a whole new level of sound control. Sounds can be connected to actions, like clicking a button. And Sounds can start a defined point in a movie, instead of just repeating in the background while a visitor views a Web site.

With Flash's sound tools, you can add a click to a button, voice narration to a presentation, and background music to an animation—all creating a fully multimedia experience for viewers of your Flash Web site or movie.

Where Do Sounds Come From?

Flash movies can incorporate sound files in the AIFF, the WAV format, or in MP3 format. In addition, if you have QuickTime version 4 or later, you can import Sound Designer II (on a Macintosh only), QuickTime (sound), Sun AU, and System 8 Sounds (on a Macintosh only) files.

Sound files in either of these formats can be imported into a Flash movie by choosing **File**, **Import**. In the Import dialog box, choose MP3, WAV (for Windows) or AIFF (for a Macintosh computer), and navigate to the folder on your system that has the sound file.

After you import a sound file, it appears in the movie library. If you widen the Library panel, you can see the actual sound files displayed as waveform, as shown in Figure 18.1.

Figure 18.1

The waveform display of a sound file gives you a rough idea of the volume variation (higher waves are louder) and the length of a sound file.

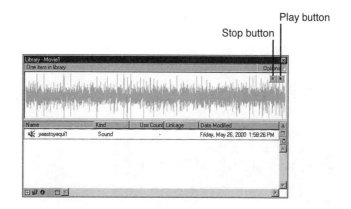

You can test sound files in the Symbol Library by clicking on the Play button in the Library panel. Click the Stop button in the Library panel to stop playing the sound file.

Music audio files can be acquired from a variety of Internet sources. Your favorite Internet search engine or portal will provide you with a list of "aiff files," or "wav files," and even "free aiff files," or "free wav files."

For example, you can download wav and aiff files at RioPop Music (BMI) http://www.riopop.com/ or Jorge Garcia, songwriter and producer, at http://www.jorge-garcia.com/. You can purchase sound effects at a reasonable price at www.sounddogs.com as well.

Use the Sounds Library

The Flash Sounds Library has dozens of sounds, like clicks, snaps, and thumps that you can experiment with. The sounds in the Sounds Library are best used with buttons. To view your options, choose **Window**, **Common Libraries**, **Sounds**.

News Flash

Music Download Issues

As I write this section of the book, the news is full of controversy over legal issues regarding the use of sound files exchanged on the Internet.

For a full discussion of legal issues involved in using music at a multimedia Web site, see the article, "The Use of Music on a Multimedia Web Site," by Ivan Hoffman, B.A., J.D. It's at http://www.ivanhoffman.com/music.html.

Do-It-Yourself Sound

There are many ways to create sound files, but most developers simply acquire pre-packaged ones.

For do-it-yourselfers, both Windows and the Mac Operating System come with fairly simple audio sound recorders. With a microphone, you can use these products to record audio files. The quality is acceptable for vocal audio (like "Hello, welcome to our Web site,") but not for music.

Backstage Pass

Recording Simple Sound Files

To record audio files on a Mac, run the SimpleSound program that comes with Mac OS.

To record an audio file on a PC, run the Sound Recorder program that comes with Windows.

With a microphone (or other input line—like from a CD player) plugged into the input or microphone jack on your computer, you can just click the Record button in the sound recorder program to capture a sound as an AIFF or WAV file (on a Macintosh with OS9, select **File**, **New**, click on the Record button and when you finish making all those silly noises, save the sound file).

Sounds Are Symbols

By now, you've noted that when you import a sound file into a Flash movie, that file enters Flash *as a symbol*. All the discussion of symbols in Chapter 10, "Recycling with Symbols," will be helpful in understanding how sounds are placed in movies.

In the rest of this chapter, I'll explain in detail how to plug a sound file into a button or a movie. But the basic concept is that you place an *instance* of a sound symbol in a frame—just like you would for a graphics symbol.

Adding Sound to Buttons

You can add a sound to the Up, Over, and/or Down state of a button. Typically sounds (like clicking noises) are added to the Down state of a button, so when a visitor clicks on a button, he or she hears a resounding "click!"

Follow these steps to add a sound to a button Down state:

Creating Buttons

In this chapter, I'll focus on adding sounds to existing buttons. For a complete explanation of how buttons work, and how to make them, jump back to Chapter 12, "Creating Control Buttons."

1. View your Library (choose **Window**, **Library**), and select an existing button in your Library, and then select **Edit** from the **Options** fly-out menu. The Symbol editing window opens, revealing the four frames that make up your button.

2. If you have sound files already imported into your movie, you can access them from the Library window you opened in step 1. If not, choose **Window**, **Common Libraries**, **Sounds** to access the clip-art sounds included with Flash (they're fine for buttons!).

3. Test the sounds in your library, or in the Sounds Library, by clicking on them in the symbol list, and then clicking the Play button in the top display area of the window. When you find a sound you like, drag that sound into the Up frame of the symbol (right onto the stage), as shown in Figure 18.2.

Figure 18.2

Drag sound files onto the stage just as you would any symbol file from the library. The sound symbol will not be visible on the stage.

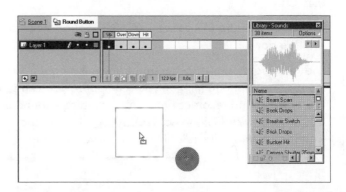

4. If you want to be sure the sound file is part of the frame, hover over the frame in the Timeline. The sound file name displays, as shown in Figure 18.3.

Figure 18.3

Figure 18.3

You can see sound files attached to frames by hovering over the frame in the Timeline. For larger movies (not buttons), it is helpful to include a separate layer for sounds.

That's it! You can test your button by clicking on the Scene link above the Layer column in the Timeline to switch to the Movie window. To test your button sound, choose **Control**, **Enable Buttons**. Drag your edited button (with it's attached sound) onto the stage, and test it by clicking on it.

Adding Sound to Movie Frames

Adding sound to movie frames is a little more complex than adding a short sound to a button frame.

You assign sound files to a movie by placing them in a keyframe. The frame you place the sound file in is the frame where the sound *starts*.

The complication is that sound file length is not determined by a number of frames, but by how large the sound file is, and how quickly it downloads in a visitor's browser and play. Therefore longer sound files are difficult to synchronize exactly with frames, and it is easiest if you can run a soundtrack for your movie that does not require that audio and visual events match exactly.

Nitty Gritty Stuff

Synchronizing Sound and Video

Synchronizing sound and video in Flash movies is pushing the edge for what we can cover in this *Complete Idiot's Guide*, but for those who want to explore that terrain, I provide a brief introduction to synchronized sound in a later section of this chapter, "Synchronizing Sound and Video."

Before you insert a sound file in a movie frame, it's best to create a separate layer for your sound. That makes it easier to keep track of where sound files are placed.

New Layers

Adding and naming new layers is covered in Chapter 8, "Working with Layers."

To place a sound in a frame in the Sound layer, select your sound layer, and click in the frame in which you will initiate the sound. Click and drag the sound symbol from your library onto the stage. As you do, the sound file will be represented in the Timeline as a waveform, starting in the frame in which you placed the file. You will see the waveform only if there are frames after the keyframe you placed the sound on.

Figure 18.4 shows a sound file in Frame 1 of the Sound layer.

Figure 18.4

The length of the sound file roughly represents the frames in which it will be played—this depends on the download time of a visitor's Internet connection.

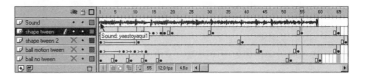

Editing Instances of Sound Files

Flash allows you to *loop* instances sound files—so that they repeat a set number of times. And, Flash allows you to *stop* sound files so they turn off when you don't want them playing anymore. Because sound files continue to play until they are done, they don't usually match your movie length at first try. Your options include extending the length of a sound file by looping (repeating) it. You can cut a sound file short by stopping it at a set frame.

Or, you can just let the sound file continue to play after the movie is completed—so the sound lasts longer than the movie.

You don't always have to edit the *sound* file to match movie and sound length. Your other option is to add, or remove frames from the movie to lengthen or shorten the movie. For example, if you are fitting a movie to a narration, or a song, you can lengthen or shorten the movie to match the sound file.

In the next section, I'll explain how to extend, and cut short, a sound file.

Looping Sound Files

If you want to extend the length of play of a sound file, you can "loop" the file so that it repeats itself. To loop a sound file, select the Frame in which the sound file is placed in the Timeline, and choose **Modify**, **Frame**. The **Sound** panel is docked with the Frame panel—click on the Sound tab to choose it.

To repeat the sound file, enter a value (greater than 0) in the Loops box in the dialog box (as shown in Figure 18.5).

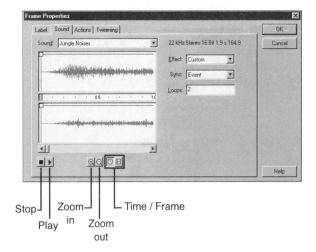

Figure 18.5

A Loop value of 0 or "1" in the Loops box of the Sound panel means the sound file will play only one time. A value of 2 repeats the sound twice, and so on.

After you loop a sound, the file will display in the Timeline as repeated waveforms (as long as there are frames in the timeline in which to display the waveform—if not, you won't see it). In Figure 18.6, the repeated sound file synchronizes nicely with the number of frames in the movie—it repeats twice each time the short movie is viewed.

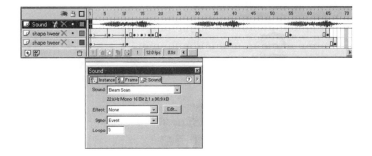

Figure 18.6

In this movie, the sound file (repeated three times) fits the movie length just right. If a sound file is too short, it can be looped. If it's too long, it can be stopped. Or...you can adjust the number of frames in the movie to match the length of the soundtrack.

Stopping Sound Files

Once started in a frame, sound files play until they are done, unless you stop them.

To stop a sound file, create a blank keyframe in a frame beyond (to the right of) the frame in which the sound starts. In the Sound panel, choose None from the Sound drop-down list.

To restart the sound, insert a keyframe, and display the Sound panel. In the Sound drop-down menu, choose the sound you wish to restart. In the Sync drop-down menu, choose Start, as shown in Figure 18.7.

219

Figure 18.7

When you start a sound file, you need to remember to choose both a sound file and the Start command in the Sound Panel.

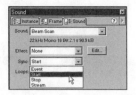

When you test your movie (choose **Control**, **Test Movie**), the sound will stop and start depending on sounds you assigned to start (or stop) in the Frame panel.

Editing Volume and Stereo Separation

Flash allows you to manage the volume for each channel of stereo sound. This allows you to not only control the volume of a sound file in playback, but also to orchestrate the relationship between the two speakers in a stereo sound system.

For example, if a sound file includes two voices, you can increase the volume in the right channel while one voice speaks, and increase the volume in the left channel while another voice speaks.

Or, you can use balance controls to create the illusion of a sound starting on one side of a movie, and ending on the other (for example, the sound of a speeding car as it races across the screen).

News Flash

Not Everyone Has Stereo

A couple of drawbacks to stereo separation: Stereo sound files are larger than mono files, so they take longer to download. Also, not all systems interpret stereo. This is especially important for worldwide media distribution, because in some parts of the world connections are slow and high-powered audio systems aren't as standard. On the other hand, when you are developing a movie for an environment where the movie will be viewed using high-quality audio equipment, stereo separation can add a component of impressive, two dimensional sound.

Using Built-In Stereo Effects

Flash comes with a bunch of cool speaker-separation effects that allow you to create sounds that fade from left to right, or right to left, play just on the right or left channel, or fade in and out.

To access these effects, select a frame with a sound file, and open the Sound panel. In the Sound panel, choose an effect from the Effect drop-down menu. In Figure 18.8, I'm assigning a fade left-to-right effect. Clicking the Edit button in the Sound Panel displays the Edit Envelope window that graphically represents the selected sound effect.

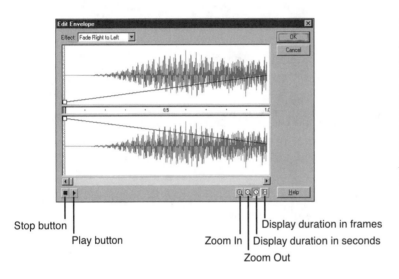

Stop button
Play button
Zoom In
Zoom Out
Display duration in frames
Display duration in seconds

Figure 18.8

As you open the Edit Envelope window, note the Stop and Play buttons on the left, the + (zoom in) and – (zoom out) icons, and the Time (clock) and Frames icons that toggle between displaying the sound in frame length and seconds.

Editing Volume and Balance

The Edit Envelope window allows you to custom tune volume and balance for sound files.

To custom define volume (and balance), drag on the boxes on the left and right end of the volume line to change volume. Drag up to increase volue in a channel for a selected segment of a sound, and drag down to decrease volume shown in Figure 18.9.

Figure 18.9

Dragging up on a portion of the volume line in a channel increases volume for that part of the sound. Clicking and dragging on a segment of the line creates an adjustable volume control point in both channels.

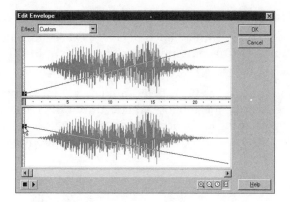

After editing (or just viewing) a sound effect in the Edit Envelope, click OK to save the sound effect and exit the Edit Envelope window.

Synchronizing Sound and Video

Flash allows you to exactly synchronize sounds files with movie frames by breaking sound files into many tiny sound files that are associated with a single frame in a movie.

By synchronizing sounds with movie frames, you can precisely define what sound will occur in a specific frame. By adding (or deleting) frames, you can create sophisticated sound/visual synchronization.

To synchronize sound files with frames, select a frame with a sound and open the Sound panel. In the Sound panel, choose Stream from the Sync drop-down menu, as shown in Figure 18.10.

Figure 18.10

Because this sound file has been synchronized with the available frames in the movie, Flash has loped off the end of the sound file at .75 seconds, so it does not extend past the end of the movie. Normal ("Event") sound files continue to play until they are done, even after a movie is over.

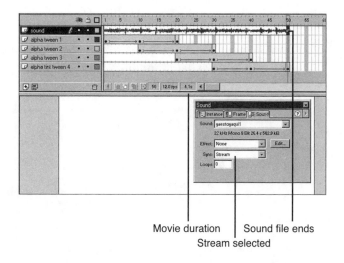

Movie duration | Sound file ends

Stream selected

When you synchronize sound, Flash will truncate (cut) the length of your sound file if necessary to fit the number of frames in your movie.

The Least You Need to Know

➤ Sound files can be imported in mp3, aiff, or wav format. Users of QuickTime can import additional sound formats.

➤ You can acquire sound files from special effects CDs, the Internet, or make them yourself. The Flash Sounds Library includes many sound files.

➤ A sound file can be attached to the Up, Over, and/or Down State of a button—try a "click" with the Down state for fun.

➤ Imported sound files are available from the movie Library, and can be placed in frames by dragging them off the symbol library and onto the stage.

➤ Flash includes tools for editing volume, length, and balance of sound files.

➤ You can synchronize sound files, breaking them into tiny files that are attached to single frames, and play together in sequence to create the original sound.

Advanced Animation Techniques

In This Chapter

➤ Adding conditional actions to frames

➤ Looping movies

➤ Launching new movies from a Flash movie

In this chapter, you'll explore some of the most sophisticated powers of Flash. You will explore how Flash can react to things like download time to control movie display. And, you'll look at how you can collect data, and then use that data to determine what movie a viewer watches.

Along the way, you'll examine the LoadMovie action, which allows you to load one Flash movie from another movie without adding anything to the HTML Web page that hosts the movie.

With this knowledge, you can create movies that collect information like a visitor's name, income, location, or budget, and then show a customized presentation based on that information.

What is that kind of thing doing in a *Complete Idiot's Guide*? Well, for one thing, we know you're not really a complete idiot at all. But beyond that, this kind of programming is manageable even for a Flash beginner.

Waiting Until a Frame Is Loaded

Sometimes elements of your Flash movie take a while to download. Large audio files and large bitmap graphics, for example, often take longer to download than Flash vector graphics. This can cause your movie to get out of synch when it plays over the Web.

For example, if you look at the Timeline for my movie in Figure 19.1, it shows a soundtrack that starts in Frame 91. The soundtrack is timed to mesh with the action in Frame 91.

Figure 19.1

Movies can be programmed so that a frame will not display until all elements are downloaded.

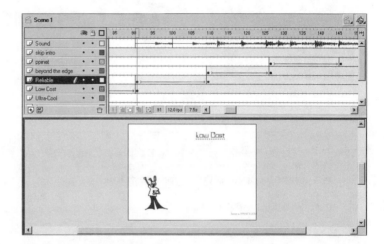

Different Download Times—Different Movies

In the example illustrated in Figure 19.1, I can loop (repeat) frames 1–90, so that they play over and over until all the elements in Frame 91 (including the large sound file) download.

If a Web browser has a fast Internet connection, my movie might not need to loop at all—by the time the movie gets to Frame 91, the sound file may already have downloaded. However, with a slow Internet connection, it might be necessary to loop the movie several times before the sound file is ready to play.

By using Flash's If Frame is Loaded action, I can have Flash determine at Frame 90 whether Frame 91 is ready to play. If so, the movie continues.

Using the If Frame Is Loaded Action

The If Frame is Loaded action is used in connection with an Else command. The Else command tells Flash what to do if the condition is not met. So, in this case, you

use the `Else` command to tell Flash to loop the beginning of the movie if Frame 91 is not yet loaded.

To use the `If Frame Is Loaded` action, follow these steps:

1. Click in a frame on your Timeline where you will insert your action, and if the frame is not already a Keyframe choose **Insert**, **Blank Keyframe**.

2. With the frame selected, select **Window**, **Actions** to open the Object Actions panel.

3. Click the Add (+) icon, and choose Actions, **ifFrameLoaded**.

4. In the Frame box of the parameter area, select the frame that you are using to test the download. In Figure 19.2, I'm setting this at Frame 91.

You're Programming!

The programming term for this is *branching*, which means that if a condition is met, the movie "branches" one way, and if it's not, the movie "branches" another way.

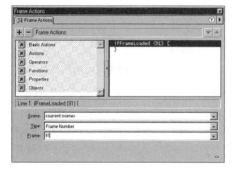

Figure 19.2

The frame number in the If Frame is Loaded *action defines the frame that must be loaded before the action takes place.*

5. With the `If Frame is Loaded` command selected, click the Add icon and choose Basic Actions, Go To. Make sure the parameter area of the Object Action panel has Go To and Play selected, as shown in Figure 19.3. In the Frame box, enter the Frame to which the movie will jump if the Frame defined in step 4 is loaded.

6. The final step is to add a command that will tell Flash what to do if the specified frame is *not* loaded. Do this by clicking the creating a new, blank keyframe *after* the keyframe that has the ifFrameLoaded action. With the new

Action Parameters

The Expand/Collapse the Parameters Area icon in the lower right corner of the Frame Actions panel displays or hides the parameters area. Many actions have definable parameters; other actions do not.

blank keyframe selected, use the add icon and choose Basic Actions, Goto. Accept the default parameter settings to send the movie back to a frame (like Frame 1).

Figure 19.3

This movie will jump to Frame 91 if all the elements in Frame 91 are downloaded into a browser.

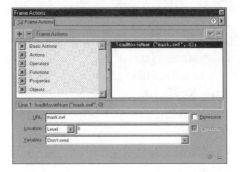

ifFrameLoaded Versus _FramesLoaded

Flash 5's revised Actionscript introduces a new action, _Framesloaded that can be programmed to accomplish pretty much the same thing as the traditional Flash ifFrameLoaded action. The main difference is that the old reliable ifFrameLoaded command is easy to use, while _FramesLoaded requires several additional actions to function.

Launching One Movie from Another Movie

You can program Flash to start one movie from another movie. For example, a Web page can have a Flash movie embedded within it. When that movie ends, the movie itself can call a new movie to start playing—without adding any code to the Web page.

Flash even gives you the option of launching your second movie *right on top* of your original movie. Layering movies this way can get kind of chaotic, but if you design your original movie so the final frame makes a nice movie background, you can use many-layered movies for some interesting effects.

Why Load Movies?

Linking movies this way is one option for managing long movies—you can edit movies one at a time, but visitors think they are watching one long movie. The process is similar to switching reels at a movie theater, so that viewers watch one long movie broken into three reels.

Among the advantages of stringing movies together is the ability to use different movie properties like background colors or frame rates.

Loading movies from within movies also allows you to create an entire Web site in Flash, without nesting your movie in additional Web pages.

Loading Movies

To load a movie from another movie, start by selecting the last frame in your movie (or another frame from which you want to launch the new movie).

View the Frame Actions Panel (choose Window, Actions). Click the Add icon and choose **Basic Actions, Load Movie**. In the URL box in the parameters area of the Frame Actions Panel, enter the Flash *.swf filename of the movie that will load. For example, in Figure 19.4, I'm loading a new movie called mask.swf.

If you want to clear the original movie and just display the new movie, change the Location value to 0.

Test your new movie link by choosing **Control**, **Test Movie**.

Level 1... or 0?

Flash considers the current movie Level 0, and a movie layered on top of that movie as Layer 1. Unless you want your movies layered on top of one another (that can be a tricky effect, but usually you don't want that), choose Layer 0.

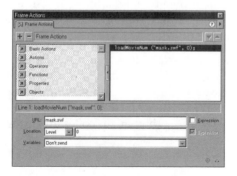

Figure 19.4

Enter the filename of the loading movie in the URL parameter box for the Load Movie *action.*

Using Variables

In Chapter 14, "Filling In the Blanks," you explored the process of collecting data in a text field. You can also collect number data. For example, you can ask a viewer for his or her zip code, age, or even income (if you're nosy).

In Chapter 14, you used collected input data to display information in a movie. For example, you can ask someone his name, and then "echo" that name in your movie, greeting a viewer with "Dave...watch this," (if your viewer's name is Dave!).

Backstage Pass

Loading Movies

You can refer back to the section in this chapter, "Launching One Movie from Another Movie," for instructions on using the Load Movie action.

Backstage Pass

Loading Movies

Instructions for creating an input field are found in the section "Creating Text Boxes" in Chapter 14. You can refer to that section for details on how to assign the actions referred to in the following instructions.

Using Variables to Load Movies

One scenario for branching based on a variable is to combine variables with the Load Movie action.

Here, you'll look at how to use collected data to actually control the content of a movie. For instance, if a viewer works in a selected department, he or she can see a movie specific to that department.

Combining an If Action with a Load Movie Action

To combine the Load Movie command with a variable, first create a text box to collect a variable. If you want to follow my example, call that variable *inputfield*.

Figure 19.5 shows the Properties dialog box for a Text Box to collect a variable called inputfield.

Add a Stop action to the frame that collects your data to allow your visitor to input data in the text box. And, add a button with an associated Play action to start the movie back up after your visitor has entered data. The frame should look something like the one in Figure 19.6.

To keep this example manageable, let's say that you have two movies you want to show—one for folks in the Eastern half of the United States, and one for folks in the West. You can use zip codes to determine which movie to show (higher zip codes are in the West, lower zip codes in the East).

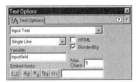

Figure 19.5

You can see—and change—Text Box properties by selecting a text box, and choosing **Text**, **Options** *The Variable area in the Text Options panel defines the field name of the data you collect in that Text Box.*

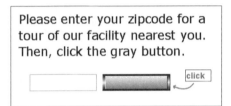

Please enter your zipcode for a tour of our facility nearest you. Then, click the gray button.

click

Figure 19.6

The text box in this frame collects data. The frame has a Stop *action assigned to allow visitors to input data. And the button has a* Play *action assigned to it to resume the movie. The collected data will be used to determine which movie to launch.*

In any frame after the one where you collect the variable data, add an action that loads a movie based on the variable data. To do that, follow these steps, and refer to Figure 19.7 as an example of using an If and an Else action to branch between two movies—East.swf, and West.swf.

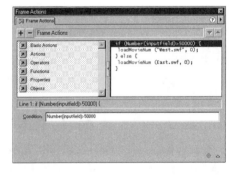

Figure 19.7

In this action, the variable inputfield is evaluated to see if the value is greater than 50000. If so, the movie West.swf loads. If not, the movie East.swf loads.

1. Select a frame after the one where the variable is collected in a text box, and open the Frame Actions panel by choosing Window, Actions.

2. Choose "+", Actions, If to generate an If action. In the Condition field of the parameter area enter the text box variable name (like inputfield).

3. Enter a comparative operator, like =, >, or <.

231

Comparative Whats?

Comparative operators allow Flash to compare the variable collected in a text box with some criteria you want to measure that variable by. For example, if the criteria is "State = Ohio," you can load a movie based on whether the variable is *equal to* Ohio. Other comparative operators include > (greater than), < (less than), >= (greater than or equal to), and <= (less than or equal to). <> means *not equal to.*

4. Follow the comparative operator with a text string (like "Ohio") or a value (like "50000").

5. Nested (indented) under the If action, add a Load Movie action with the movie to be loaded if the If statement is correct.

6. Add an Else action.

7. Under the Else action, nest (indent) a LoadMovie action and add the movie that plays for everyone else in the URL parameter.

8. Your script should look something like the one in Figure 19.7. You can test your movie using **Control**, **Test Movie**.

Troubleshooting Your Branching Load Movie Script

Script doesn't work? Here are a few things to check: Make sure you have movies that match the filename in your LoadMovie actions and that they are saved in the same folder as the movie that launches them. Make sure that your movie collects a variable in a frame preceding the frame with the LoadMovie action. And check to see that you used the exact same variable name in the text box and in the Action script.

The branching possibilities with Action scripts are almost endless, and go well beyond the scope of this book. But if you're comfortable with a bit of programming (and specifically JavaScript—which is very close to Flash's Action script), code away.

The Least You Need to Know

➤ You can create a Flash movie that pauses or loops (repeats) until all elements have downloaded. This is helpful in synchronizing soundtracks with visuals, or delaying a movie until large bitmap images have downloaded.

➤ You can use the LoadMovie action to launch one movie from another movie. The second movie can be shown literally "on top of" the first movie, or it can be shown in place of the first movie.

➤ You can use If and Else actions to load different movies based on data collected in variables.

Part 7
Flashing the Web

You've created a great Flash animation—now the problem is to get it into a form where other people can see it!

In the following chapters, you'll learn how to combine objects created by other programs with Flash movies, how to get Flash movies into Web sites, and how to make Flash movies available in other formats. By the time we're done, you'll be able to make your movie accessible to anyone.

Getting Outside Help: Importing Objects

In This Chapter

➤ Importing vector graphics into Flash

➤ Importing bitmaps into Flash

➤ Tracing bitmaps for efficient vector images

➤ Importing text

Considering that Flash is also a powerful animation and movie design program, it has a pretty cool set of tools. But it is not *mainly* a drawing program, and for high-powered illustration, you will want to integrate drawings from other programs like Adobe PhotoShop or Macromedia Freehand.

In this chapter I'll show you how to do that.

Along with importing vector graphics images from drawing programs, you are likely to encounter bitmap images that are included in your movie or Web design project. If you've read many of the preceding chapters, you've gotten a sense that Flash is a *vector* graphics environment. That is, Flash uses a memory-efficient system based on mathematical formulas to define graphics.

In this chapter, you'll explore two options for imported bitmap images: Incorporate them as memory-hogging bitmaps in your Flash movie (sometimes necessary), or convert them to vector images.

Importing Vector Graphics into Flash

Flash isn't the only graphics program that uses vector file formats to create and save graphics images. Other popular drawing packages include Macromedia's own Freehand, Adobe Illustrator, CorelDRAW, and various technical drawing programs that save files to the AutoCAD *.dxf format. In addition, the *.wmf (Windows Metafile) format is used by Windows to copy and paste vector graphics.

When you import a drawing saved to a vector graphics format, you can then edit it in Flash as if you had created it with Flash's drawing tools.

Importing Vector Graphics

To import a vector graphic into an active (unlocked) layer in an open movie, choose **File**, **Import**. As you do that, the Import dialog box opens, as shown in Figure 20.1.

Figure 20.1

If you choose All Formats from the Files of Type drop-down menu in the Import dialog box, Flash will display all files that have importable file formats.

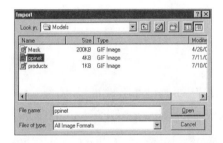

In the Import dialog box, navigate to the folder with your file, and choose the file format of your file from the File of Type drop-down menu. Then double-click on the file.

Can't Import?

Are you trying to import a file and finding the **File**, **Import** menu option grayed out? Troubleshooting step one: make sure your active layer is *unlocked*. If the active layer is locked, you can't import into it.

After you import a file, it appears on the stage in the active frame of your movie. Imported vector images enter Flash as grouped objects. To reduce them to individual objects for editing, select the imported grouped object, and choose Modify, Break Apart. Now you can edit your imported vector objects just as you would a drawing you created in Flash.

Copying and Pasting Vector Graphics

If you find a vector graphics image that you can't import into Flash because it's not in a supported import format, you can always use the Clipboard to move it

into Flash. I do this a lot, because I use CorelDRAW to create drawings, and DRAW's *.cdr format isn't a supported vector import type.

When you copy a vector graphic onto the Clipboard from another program, make sure you select the entire drawing in the original program. Then, simply choose **Edit**, **Copy** from that program's menu bar.

To paste a file into an active layer in an open Flash movie, choose **Edit**, **Paste Special**. Depending on your operating system, and the origin of your file, you will have different options in the Paste Special dialog box in Flash, as shown in Figure 20.2.

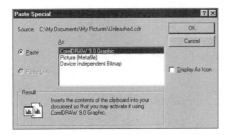

Figure 20.2

Because the drawing in the Clipboard was originally created in CorelDRAW, the Clipboard offers the option of pasting it into Flash as a DRAW object. If I chose that option, I could reopen the file in DRAW for editing by double-clicking on it.

The options you are offered in the Paste Special dialog box basically amount to two different options (with different variations within them). Those options are vector or bitmap. If you choose the bitmap option, your imported drawing will come into Flash as a bitmap file. For a full discussion of how to handle imported bitmaps, see the section "Importing Bitmap Files," a bit later in this chapter.

Other options, like "Picture (Metafile)," bring images into Flash as grouped vector images that can be broken apart (by choosing **Modify**, **Break Apart**), and edited just like Flash drawings.

Importing Bitmap Files

James Brown used to sing, "This is a man's world." Maybe. Maybe not. But we Flash users must live in what is still, mainly, a bitmap world.

Backstage Pass

If at First You Don't Succeed...

Importing via the Clipboard is a bit unpredictable. Always use **Paste Special** instead of just **Copy**, **Paste** so you can see what your options are. You can experiment with different vector import options when there is more than one available.

Bitmaps, which are defined by storing data on every pixel in the image, include the globally accepted GIF (pronounced with either a hard or soft g) and JPEG ("jay-peg"). As a Flash developer, expect to be given files in all kinds of bitmap formats, including Photoshop's PSD format, the PNG (pronounced "ping") format, and the generic PostScript format (EPS).

Flash Imports EPS—Sort Of

The Encapsulated PostScript file format is a widely used format for preparing graphics for printed output. I've had mixed experiences trying to import EPS files created in other programs besides Freehand. However, Freehand can open most EPS files, and export them to bitmap or vector formats that are more easily imported into Flash.

To import a bitmap image, choose **File**, **Import**. The Import dialog box opens. Choose All Image Formats from the Files of Type drop-down menu in the Import dialog box, so that Flash will display all files that have importable graphic file formats.

Looking for All Graphic Files Versus Some Graphic Files

If you are looking for a file, and not sure which file format it is in, use the All Image Format type to see all graphic files. If you have many files in a folder, and want to screen for a specific file type, choose the file format from the File of Type drop-down menu.

Double-click on a file to import it into the selected frame and layer in Flash.

Alternately, you can bring a copied bitmap image into Flash by choosing **Edit**, **Paste Special**, and selecting a bitmap format from the Paste Special dialog box, as shown in Figure 20.3.

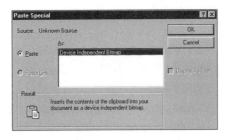

Figure 20.3

Bitmap images copied to the Clipboard can only be pasted into Flash as bitmaps.

Imported bitmap images can be moved, rotated, and scaled just like Flash drawings. However, you cannot use the Erase, Paint Bucket, or Ink Bottle tools to modify bitmaps.

Color Cropping Bitmap Images with the Color Wand

Flash allows you to strip colors from imported bitmaps using the Color Wand modifier in the Lasso tool. For example, if you import a picture with a background, you often want to strip the background from the picture.

To use the Color Wand, follow these steps:

1. Select a bitmap and choose **Modify**, **Break Apart**.

2. With the Arrow tool, click *outside* the bitmap to deselect it.

3. Choose the Lasso tool, and click the Magic Wand Properties icon in the Options area of the Toolbox. This opens the Magic Wand Settings dialog box, as shown in Figure 20.4.

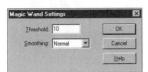

Figure 20.4

Magic Wand settings determine how discriminating Flash will be in selecting colors to delete from a bitmap.

4. The Magic Wand Settings dialog box allows you to define two things—how close a color match you want to use to select a color in the bitmap, and what kind of edging you want to use for the cutout section of the bitmap. Choose a Threshold setting.

Figure 20.5 shows the effect of different Threshold settings in stripping the black background off an imported flower bitmap.

Magic Wand Settings

A low Threshold setting selects only color pixels that are very close to each other. A high Threshold setting is very indiscriminate, and selects all color pixels that are close to the selected pixel color.

After you determine a good Threshold setting (through trial and error), you can fine-tune your Magic Wand cutout by experimenting with the four options in the Smoothing drop-down menu.

5. Click on the Magic Wand modifier in the Lasso toolbar, and move the wand over a color in a bitmap graphic, as shown in Figure 20.6. Click to select that color in the image.

6. You can move or delete this region just as you would any other selected drawing object in Flash, as shown in Figure 20.7. To delete the selected color, press Delete to delete that color from the image.

Figure 20.5

Color Threshold settings range from 1–200. High settings will strip all dark colors out of this picture, not just the black background.

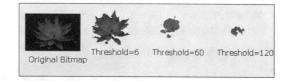

Figure 20.6

Selecting a color region with the Magic Wand.

Figure 20.7

After a color region is selected with the Magic Wand, it becomes a distinct graphics object that can be edited (or deleted).

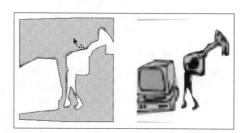

Converting Bitmaps to Flash Vector Graphics

You can work with imported bitmap images in Flash. The downside to this is that those bitmaps greatly increase the size of your Flash file, and cut against Flash's speedy vector-based downloading.

Nitty Gritty Stuff

How Bitmaps Become Vectors

Flash's vector graphics are defined as curves and lines as you generate them. In order to translate an existing bitmap image into a vector graphic, Flash has to "figure out" how to convert a bunch of dots (pixels) into defined lines and curves. For this reason, converting bitmaps into vectors often requires much trial-and-error, and experimenting with different settings.

To convert a bitmap into a bunch of Flash shapes, follow these steps:

1. Select the Bitmap in your Flash movie.

2. Choose **Modify**, **Trace Bitmap** from the menu bar. The Trace Bitmap dialog box appears, as shown in Figure 20.8.

Figure 20.8

The Trace Bitmap dialog box allows you to define how Flash will transform a bitmap into a bunch of vector objects.

3. In the Color Threshold box, enter a high number to create more shapes, a low number to create fewer.

4. In the Minimum Area box, enter a higher value to create fewer vector shapes, a low number to allow Flash to generate very small shapes (resulting in lots of shapes from your bitmap).

5. Use the Curve Fit box to define how much to smooth out the outlines in the vector shapes that are generated by the trace.

6. Use the Corner Threshold box to define what kind of corners to generate for the vector shapes—many, normal, or few.

7. After you make selections in the Trace Bitmap dialog box, click **OK** to transform your bitmap into many vector graphics shapes.

If at First You Don't Succeed...

Tracing takes time. After all, Flash is analyzing your bitmap image, and figuring out a logical way to convert all those pixels into lines and shapes. No easy task. So prepare to take a break during complex traces.

And, prepare to do some experimenting. Tracing is not an exact science, and it usually requires a few tries to convert your bitmap into a Flash vector object. The result is often a strikingly improved image.

Converting bitmap images to vectors often creates interesting graphic effects, like the converted bitmap in Figure 20.9.

Figure 20.9

This bitmap was con- verted to vectors, allowing each element of the graphic to be edited.

Bitmap version   Vector version

The vector image can be edited using all the Flash drawing tools. And, it can be en- larged with out the distortion that affects an enlarged bitmap image.

Importing Text

While we're discussing importing files, I'd like to say a quick word on importing text.

Flash does not allow you to import Word files (or files from other word processors). But you can copy and paste files from Word or any word processor into Flash *as text objects*.

To import text, select the text in your word processor, and copy it to the Clipboard (**Edit**, **Copy**). Then, choose **Edit**, **Paste Special** in Flash (with an unlocked layer selected).

The Paste Special dialog box will display options allowing you to paste your text as ASCII text, or to preserve the format of your word processor (see Figure 20.10).

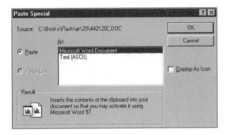

Figure 20.10

*Don't choose **Edit**, **Paste**—choose **Edit**, **Paste Special**—so you can define how you want to import copied text.*

If you choose to import text as a Word (or other word processor) object, you format and edit the text by double-clicking on it to *open the text in the original word processor*. This can be kind of confusing. It's easier to paste the text as ASCII text. This way you can use the Text tool in Flash to edit your imported text.

The Least You Need to Know

➤ You can import drawings from other vector-based drawing programs (like Adobe Illustrator) into Flash, and edit them just as you would a Flash drawing.

➤ You can import bitmap drawings into Flash as well, from programs like Adobe PhotoShop. However, imported bitmaps slow down your Flash movie.

➤ You can convert imported bitmap images to Flash vector drawings.

➤ You can import text, and edit and format it in Flash if you use **Paste, Special** in the **Edit** menu, and choose to import the text as ASCII text.

Putting Flash Online

In This Chapter

➤ Saving Flash movies

➤ Creating Web pages with embedded Flash movies

➤ Handling browsers that don't like Flash

You don't need Flash to watch a Flash movie. All you need is a program called Flash Player. The folks at Macromedia make the Viewer available for free, both as a stand-alone program and a plug-in program that works with Web browsers like Internet Explorer and Netscape Navigator to let folks watch your movies at Web sites.

Preparing a movie for viewing starts with saving your Flash (*.fla) file as a Flash Player (*.swf) file. SWF files can be opened and viewed by anyone with the Flash Player program.

Watching Movies with Flash Player

After you have saved your file as a Flash Player file, it's ready for the world. You can post it on a Web site, put it on a CD, or send it over the Web. And anyone who has the free Flash Player can watch it.

First step, though, is to save your Flash movie as an *.swf file.

Flash Player Files

Flash movies have a filename extension of *.fla. They can only be opened with Flash. Flash Player files are special files that can be *viewed* even by people who do not have Flash. Flash Player files have a file extension of (*.swf).

Saving Flash Player Files

There are two ways to save a Flash movie file as a Flash Player file—publish, or export. Both options create the same thing—an *.swf file that can be opened in the Flash Player. To export a Flash movie to a Flash Player movie, follow these steps:

1. Open the file in Flash.

2. Choose **File**, **Export Movie**.

3. In the Export Movie dialog box, choose Flash Player (*.swf) from the Save as Type drop-down menu, as shown in Figure 21.1.

Figure 21.1

SWF is the file format used for movies that can be played with the Flash Player.

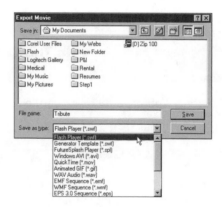

4. Navigate to the folder to which you want to save your file in the Save In drop-down menu in the Export Movie dialog box. Then, enter a filename for your Flash Player movie in the File Name area of the Export Movie dialog box, and click OK to save.

You can also create a Flash Player file for an open Flash movie by choosing **File**, **Publish** from the menu bar. This option doesn't allow you to change the filename or choose a folder like the Export option does. It automatically uses the same folder and filename your Flash movie was saved to.

Watching Movies with Flash Player

After you have saved a movie as an SWF (Flash Player) file, you can open it with the Flash Player. Or an even faster way is to launch the Flash Player by double-clicking on

an SWF file in your system's file manager program.

To open a movie from within the Flash Player, choose **File**, **Open** from the menu. The Open dialog box (shown in Figure 21.2) allows you to enter a URL if the file is on the Web, or you can use the Browse button to locate a movie on your local system.

The Flash Player's View menu provides zoom options. When you zoom in, the mouse cursor becomes a grabber hand that allows you to see different parts of the movie in the Viewer screen. The Control menu allows you to Play, Rewind, Step Forward or Backward, and turn Loop (continuous play) on or off, as shown in Figure 21.3.

Flash Player Files

What's with the SWF filename extension for playable Flash movies? SWF comes from Shock Wave File. The Shock Wave Player is another name used by Macromedia for the Flash Player.

Figure 21.2

You can open Flash movies on your own computer, or enter a URL in the Open dialog box to open movies on Web sites.

Figure 21.3

Audiences who watch your movie with the Flash Player can stop, start, rewind, and step through your movie.

In addition to watching saved movies with the Flash Player, you activate a special version of the Flash Player when you open a movie in Flash and choose **Control**, **Test Movie** from the menu bar. When you do this, the Flash Player is automatically opened, and the movie runs in the viewer.

Figure 21.4

*When you launch a Flash movie from Flash, you get additional options not available to normal movie viewers. For example, you can display the Controller in the Flash Player (choose **Window**, **Toolbars**, **Controller** from the menu bar) to rewind, play, or step through a movie.*

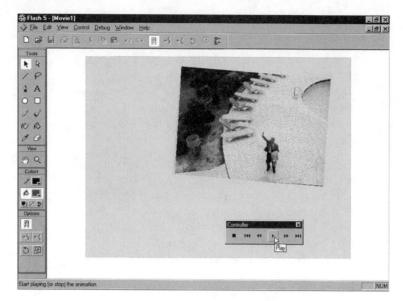

Downloading the Flash Player

If you have Flash, you already have the Flash Player. But if you are preparing Flash files for distribution, you might want to be able to clue your viewers in to where they can get the Player.

The Flash Player program can be downloaded free at

```
http://www.macromedia.com/software/flash/download/
```

Creating Web Pages with Embedded Flash Files

Backstage Pass

Flash Player Files

While creating and publishing Web sites is beyond the scope of this book, you'll find *The Complete Idiot's Guide to Creating a Web Page* a handy companion to this book when it comes to creating Web sites.

The most universal way of distributing Flash movies is over the Web. Current Web browser versions can open Flash SWF files directly. For example, the movie in Figure 21.5 is just an SWF file, open in Internet Explorer.

Adding a Flash Movie to a Web Site: The Easiest Way

You can add a Flash SWF movie file to your Web site *simply* by transferring the file to your site using whatever FTP (File Transfer Protocol) or Web Publishing program or tool you normally use.

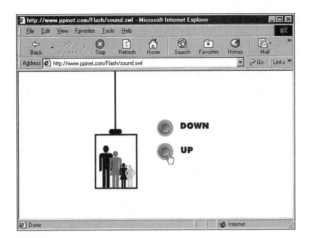

Figure 21.5

The file in the Internet Explorer title bar is not an HTML file; it's an SWF file. IE has no problem opening and displaying this file.

Nitty Gritty Stuff

Who Can See Flash Movies?

Can anyone see Flash movies in their browser? No, they can't. For advice on how to prepare Flash movies for Flashless browsers and systems, see Chapter 22, "Exporting Flash Movies."

However, the number of systems and browsers that *do* come with the ability to present Flash movies is fairly impressive. Flash movies saved to the SWF format are accessible to users of Windows 95/98, the MacOS 8.X, Internet Explorer CD, America Online, and Netscape Navigator. These programs come with a Shockwave (Flash) viewer built-in.

The uploaded Flash movie can be linked to other pages in a Web site, and will play for visitors who's browsers support Flash *.swf files, or who have the Flash viewer on their systems.

Uploading Flash *.swf files is the most no-frills way to include a Flash movie in a Web site. However, many developers will want to combine Flash movies with HTML (Web pages). This requires embedding a Flash movie in a Web page.

Embedding a Flash Movie in a Web Page

HTML is the language of the Web. It is the code by which Web browsers detect text format, graphics images, and yes... Flash movies.

Flash enables you to create Web pages that have Flash movies embedded in them.

When you embed a Flash movie in an HTML page, you can control the size of the movie. For example, the Flash movies in Figure 21.6 take up only small sections of the page.

Figure 21.6

Because the three Flash movie are embedded in an HTML page, they can share the page with other content, like text.

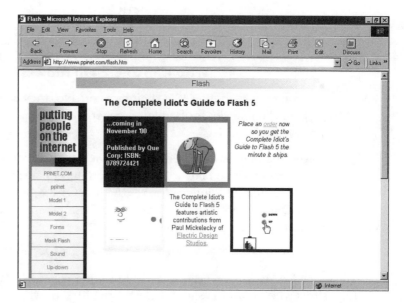

Even if you don't know any HTML, Flash will generate an HTML page with an embedded Flash movie for you. Here's how:

1. With your already saved Flash movie open, choose **File**, **Publish Settings**. The Publish Settings dialog box will open.

2. In the list of check boxes on the **Formats** tab, choose both Flash (.swf) and HTML (.html), as shown in Figure 21.7.

Nitty Gritty Stuff

What's HTML and What's It Got to Do with Flash?

HyperText Markup Language (HTML) is the common language that allows Web browsers to interpret and display text and graphics. HTML *alone* is not sufficient to display Flash movies—that requires a plug-in or a browser (like Internet Explorer) that comes ready to play Flash movies.

One approach to Web design (touted, not surprisingly by the PR folks at Macromedia) is to design an *all* Flash site. The limitation of this approach is that you cannot combine accessible, easy to edit HTML with Flash movies. The other option, which we are exploring now, is to combine Flash animated and interactive movies with pages that are primarily designed in HTML.

For a solid introduction to Web page design with HTML, check out Elizabeth Castro's *HTML for the World Wide Web.*

You can also generate HTML Web pages without knowing HTML, using programs like Dreamweaver or FrontPage.

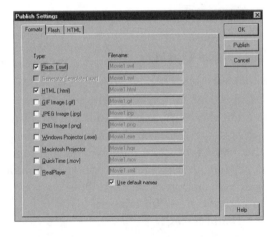

Figure 21.7

Choosing the HTML check box tells Flash to generate an HTML page with an embedded Flash movie. Filenames (and folders) are set by the name you originally assigned your Flash file, unless you deselect the Uses Default Names check box.

3. To define the generated HTML page, click on the **HTML** tab in the Publish Settings dialog box. The HTML tab is shown in Figure 21.8.

Figure 21.8

Often, you will want to simply accept Flash's default HTML settings to create a Web page with a Flash movie embedded. Once you generate that page, you can edit it with your own HTML code, or Web page editors like Dreamweaver and FrontPage that allow you to further define how the Flash movie will be displayed.

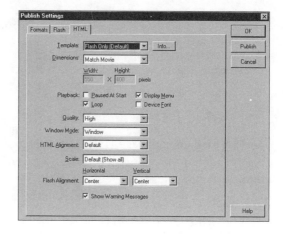

4. In the **Template** drop-down menu, either leave the selection as **Flash Only**, or choose one of the other options for presenting your movie on a Web page. Generally, the Flash Only option is a good way to make your movie accessible to modern browsers.

Nitty Gritty Stuff

Template Options

The Template drop-down menu allows you to choose from a set of HTML pages in which you can embed your Flash movie. Of course, after generating the HTML page in Flash, you can open and edit the HTML page in your favorite HTML editing program, or by adding hand-coded HTML. The Flash Only template generates a Web page that displays the movie for browsers and systems that support the Flash player. Flash 5 does the same thing, but provides an option of displaying only a picture for browsers that do not support Flash. Flash Only is a good option for most viewers. For more discussion of options for browsers that don't support Flash, see Chapter 22, "Exporting Flash Movies."

5. Use the Dimensions drop-down menu to choose whether you want to match the size of the embedded movie viewer with the movie (Match Movie), or define

a size in Pixels, or Percent. If you choose Pixels or Percent, use the Width and Height boxes to define the size of the movie in the Web page.

6. Use the Playback check boxes to define how to present the Flash movie in your Web page. The options are:

   ➤ **Playback**—Use check boxes to select any or all of the four playback check boxes.

   ➤ **Paused at Start**—Requires a viewer to start the movie by clicking a button in the movie or by choosing **Play** from the context menu.

   ➤ **Loop**—Repeats the movie endlessly.

   ➤ **Display Menu**—Makes the context menu available when visitors right-click in Windows or Command-click on a Macintosh.

   ➤ **Device Font**—Only works with viewers using Windows, and allows anti-aliased (smoothed) fonts to be used when the font in your movie is not available on a viewer's system.

7. Use the **Quality** drop-down menu to define how much anti-aliasing (smoothing of jaggedy edges) you need. More Quality (smoothing) produces nicer artwork and text, but can slow down playback speed.

8. The Window Mode drop-down menu allows you to use features only available in Internet Explorer 4.0 and higher to allow Flash movies to appear "on top of" other page elements.

Absolutely Positioned Page Objects

Absolutely positioned page objects are a rather unreliable element of HTML. They fall in the category of DHTML, or Dynamic HTML—one of the more browser-unfriendly ways to add content to a page (better to use Flash for these kinds of animated and positioned page objects!). If you're exploring that frontier, you might avail yourself of the Opaque Windowless menu option to place Flash movies on top of other objects, or the Transparent Windowless option to place movies on top of other page objects allowing those objects "under" the movie to be partly visible. If all this sounds confusing, relax—stick with the Window option; it's all you need.

9. Use the HTML Alignment drop-down menu to position the Flash movie window in the browser window. Default centers the movie; Left or Right aligns the movie on either side of the browser window. Top and bottom align the movie at the top or bottom of the browser window.

10. The Scale drop-down menu is only relevant if you defined a movie display window in the Dimensions area that is different than the size of the movie.

Different Movie and Display Sizes

In almost every case, you will want your entire movie to display in an HTML page. However, you can define a movie area in the HTML page that is smaller than the movie itself. If you do define a different movie display size in your HTML page, the Default (Show all) option fits the entire movie into the space defined in the Dimensions area of the dialog box, while maintaining the original height-to-width ratio of the movie. The No Border option scales the movie to fill the specified area while maintaining the original height-to-width ratio of the movie. If you use this option, part of the movie might be cropped out of the display window. The Exact Fit option squeezes the movie into the space defined in the Dimensions area of the dialog box. If you choose this option, your movie may have the height-to-width ratio distorted.

11. Use the Flash Alignment drop-down menus to define where to display a movie when the defined movie area is larger than the movie. For example, the movie in Figure 21.9 has been aligned to the bottom-right corner of the browser window.

12. Click the **Show Warning Messages** check box to have display error messages *in Flash* (for you, the Flash developer) if there are potential conflicts between the different HTML options you selected in the HTML tab of the Publish Settings dialog box.

13. After defining your HTML settings, click **Publish** in the Publish Settings dialog box, and click **OK** to close the dialog box.

Figure 21.9

Because the defined size of the movie is larger than the browser area, and because the alignment of the movie is the bottom-right corner of the movie area, scroll bars are necessary to see the entire movie, and some of the movie is "hidden" until a visitor scrolls down and right.

Once you have generated an HTML page with your movie embedded in it, you can upload that Web page to your server, and the whole world can see it. Be sure to upload your Flash movie (*.swf) file to the same folder/directory in your server, so that it is available to fit into your Web page.

Hand Coding HTML for Flash Movies

If you are an experienced HTML coder (and nobody says you have to be to use Flash!), you can create your own Web pages that will embed a Flash movie.

Backstage Pass

What If I Just Want My Flash Movie Inside an HTML Page?

If all you want to do is generate an HTML Web page with your Flash movie inside it, simply accept the defaults in the HTML tab of the Publish Settings dialog box, and click on **Publish**.

The <EMBED> command inserts a Flash movie in a page. The <WIDTH> and <HEIGHT> commands define the size of the movie window. You'll find more details on how to use these commands, as well as commands like <LOOP>, <ALIGN>, and <AUTOSTART> in your favorite HTML coding manual.

For Macintosh viewers, the <OBJECT> HTML tag is used to define your Flash movie.

You only need to be sure that you have placed your Flash Movie in the same Web directory as the HTML page that calls the movie.

Hand Coding for Complete Idiots

The easiest way to combine a Flash movie with your own HTML coding is to generate the HTML in Flash, and then add to it in your HTML editor or with HTML hand coding.

Testing Your Movie in a Web Page

After you have defined your HTML settings, you can view your movie in your system's default browser by pressing the F12 function key, or by choosing **File**, **Publish Preview**, **HTML**.

Flash will launch your default system browser and open the HTML page that displays your movie. You'll see that in addition to HTML code that embeds your movie, Flash generated a title for your page (displayed in your browser title bar). That title is based on your Flash filename.

Feel free to explore the HTML code in your page by choosing **View**, **Page Source** in Netscape Navigator, or **View**, **Source** in Internet Explorer. Figure 21.10 shows HTML code generated by a Flash movie.

The Least You Need to Know

➤ Flash movies can be viewed from within Flash or with the Flash Player.

➤ Flash movies are often displayed in Web pages and can be viewed by current Web browsers without any additional utilities.

➤ Flash will generate the HTML code needed to display your Flash movie in a Web page.

➤ The Web pages generated by Flash can be edited, either by changing the HTML code by hand, or by opening those files in an HTML editor program (like Dreamweaver, FrontPage, or Netscape Composer).

Exporting Flash Movies

In This Chapter

➤ Why export?

➤ Exporting Flash static graphics

➤ Exporting static graphic sequences

➤ Exporting Flash animation

➤ Exporting sound

One of the coolest things about Flash is how widely accepted it is. Internet Explorer 5 (and later) comes equipped to run Flash movies. And Netscape Navigator users can download the Flash/Shockwave player (once again the URL is http://www.macromedia.com/shockwave/).

Trouble is, some folks don't have a current version of Internet Explorer. Or they might not want to download the Flash/Shockwave player plug-in for Netscape.

And new technologies are emerging that don't yet support Flash movies—like Linux Web browsers, Web TV, and other new ways of connecting to the Web.

In short, Flash maybe widely accepted, but it's not quite global yet. And you still might want to export movies, static graphics, and extracted sound files to more universally used file formats in order to communicate with your viewers.

In this chapter, you'll explore how to save Flash movies as movies in other formats, as static graphics, and how to pull sound files out of movies and save them as separate files. And we'll discuss what format works best, when.

Exporting Flash Movies to Static Graphics

You can grab a single frame of a Flash movie and save it as a static graphic. For example, in Figure 22.1, I've set up my screen to save Frame 10 of my movie.

Figure 22.1

Note that Frame 10 is selected in the Timeline— only this frame will be exported as a static graphic.

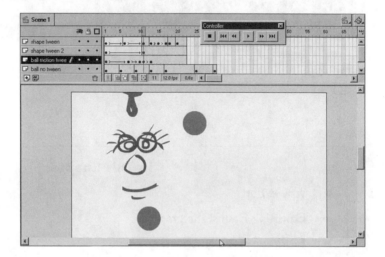

Nitty Gritty Stuff

What About Hidden Layers?

When you export a frame in Flash, you export *all layers* in that frame, whether they are shown or hidden. This can get confusing if you have hidden a layer—you might wonder where the extra stuff came from in your exported graphic. For that reason, it's useful to select Show for All Layers (using the Show/Hide All icon) before exporting a frame as a static graphic.

After you have selected the frame you want to export, choose **File**, **Export Image** from the menu. The Export Image dialog box appears, as shown in Figure 22.2.

Figure 22.2

Use the Export Image dialog box to choose a filename, a folder, and a format for your exported image.

Use the **Save In** drop-down menu to navigate to a folder on your system. Enter a filename for your exported file in the File Name box. In the **Save as Type** drop-down menu, choose a file format.

Choosing a File Format for Export

If you want to export a frame of a Flash movie to be displayed on the Web, your basic options are GIF and JPEG. I'll go into how and when to use those formats in some detail a bit later in this chapter, but first, let me introduce all the static graphic export formats available:

➤ **Metafile (EMF and WMF)**—Use this format (also called *Windows* Metafile) for printed documents created in Windows.

➤ **Postscript (EPS)**—Encapsulated PostScript is one of the most widely recognized file formats for hardcopy printing.

➤ **Adobe Illustrator (AI)**—The AI file format is shared by Illustrator and Macromedia Freehand, and can be imported by CorelDRAW—so this is a convenient format for all vector graphics programs.

➤ **AutoCad (DXF)**—Sharing your image with an architect or draftsman? Then this is a good format for export.

➤ **Bitmap (BMP)**—Widely interpreted bitmap graphic format.

➤ **JPEG (JPG/JPEG)**—One of the two (along with GIF) Web-compatible file formats. JPEG preserves colors better than GIF (use JPEGs for Gradient Fills). JPEG format does not allow transparent colors or interlacing—a technique that "fades in" large images as they download.

➤ **GIF**—The other Web-compatible graphics file formats (along with JPEG). GIF does not preserve colors as well as JPEG, but allows interlacing.

➤ **PNG**—Okay, I lied—there is a third Web Compatible graphics file format—but it's not *that* universally interpreted by browsers. PNG is similar to GIF format.

Of the various export options, you will use GIF and JPEG for graphics destined for Web sites. Different file formats will provide different export options.

261

Export Options

Most export file formats have a few options in common. You can decide whether to save the whole screen as an exported image, or just the picture. Many export formats allow you to define exact dimensions for your exported image.

You can also determine how many colors to export. More colors mean more accuracy in how colors are reproduced in your exported image, but more colors also increase file size (and download time).

Many export formats have a Smooth check box. Select Smooth to eliminate "jaggies" in angles that make your diagonal lines look like steps.

To export just the image (and not the full background size), choose **Minimum Image Area** from the **Include** drop-down menu. To export the entire stage area, choose **Full Document Size** from the drop-down menu.

If you want to custom define the exact size of the area you want to export, enter dimensions in the Width and Height boxes.

You can define a resolution for your exported graphic by changing the value in the Resolution box—72 dpi is standard resolution for graphics destined for computer screens (including for Web sites). Higher resolutions are used for hardcopy printed images.

More Colors with Dithering

What happens when you save an image with 500 colors in 8 bit color? The "missing" colors that are not included in an 8 bit (256 color) palette are "faked" in your image by mixing together pixels of colors that *are* part of the palette.

Color depth options define how many colors are saved in your exported graphic. The 8 bit color option saves your image with 256 colors. For most Web graphics, 8 bit color is plenty.

You can also export images using a 24-bit palette. This saves a total spectrum of color—about 16 million colors. Use 24 bit only when exporting images for hardcopy printing.

Exporting to GIF

If you export to a GIF image, you can add interlacing to your picture. Interlacing a GIF file entertains browsers while the file downloads by having the picture resolve itself in more and more detail, rather than just "dropping down" from top to bottom as the file downloads into a browser.

The GIF export format also allows transparency—which means that the background of an image (usually white, unless you have configured a different movie background color) will not show up when the image is placed on a Web page.

Figure 22.3 shows Interlacing and Transparency selected for an exported GIF image.

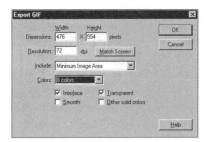

Figure 22.3

By choosing eight colors, you are minimizing the size of the exported GIF file.

Figure 22.4 shows the exported GIF image embedded in a Web site.

Figure 22.4

Because this image was exported as a GIF with a transparent background, the image appears to sit right on top of the page background.

Exporting to JPEG

When you export images that include a lot of color nuances (gradient fills or photos), you can often preserve the colors better by exporting an image to JPEG format.

The Export JPEG dialog box includes an option to regulate image quality. Higher image quality (the highest being 100) creates images that are larger in file size, slower to download, and more accurate. Low quality images download faster, but look worse. It often takes some experimenting to determine what level of compression works best—as shown in Figure 22.5.

Figure 22.5

The high quality JPEG was exported using a quality setting of 100. It is 5MB in size. The low quality JPEG was exported using a quality setting of 1. Its size is 4MB. Not much of a savings in download time considering the loss of quality.

Exporting to Graphic Sequences

Flash gives you two basic export options—you can export to a static graphic (like GIF or JPEG files), or you can export to other movie formats (like QuickTime, or AVI).

Exporting to graphic sequences lies somewhere in between those two options. Graphic sequences export each frame of your movie to a separate static graphics file.

Exporting to graphic sequences is similar to exporting images—except that Flash generates an image for *every frame* in a movie.

To generate a graphic sequence from an open movie, choose **File**, **Export Movie**. In the **Save as Type** drop-down menu in the Export Movie dialog box, choose one of the sequence options (like JPEG Sequence or GIF Sequence). Enter a filename and click **Save** to generate an image for each frame in your movie.

Generating graphic sequences can be helpful when you are presenting a hardcopy outline of a movie to a client. Figure 22.6 shows a display of generated images from a movie.

Figure 22.6

Presenting five frames can convey the general action sequence of a movie—as these five frames do.

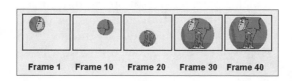

Frame 1   Frame 10   Frame 20   Frame 30   Frame 40

Backstage Pass

That's a Lotta Images!

A little quick calculating tells you that a 400 frame movie will generate a heck of a lot of static graphics—400 to be exact. So, for large movies, graphic sequences are not usually a practical option. You can use graphic sequences to generate prints from your movie—kind of like the old-fashioned animation plates that were hand-drawn for cartoons.

One option is to use only *some* of your generated sequential images. For example, you could use only every tenth image in a 100 frame movie, and put together a short-hand version of the movie. In Figure 22.6 that follows, I stripped a longer movie down to five generated images.

Exporting to Other Movie Formats

Flash is quite open-minded about movie file formats. Although the folks at Macromedia continue their campaign to have Flash's Shockwave viewer adopted by the whole world, they also realize that many potential Flash movie viewers rely on other movie viewers instead.

No problem. Flash can export movies to all the widely used movie viewer formats, including Macintosh's QuickTime format, Windows' AVI format, and the animated GIF format that is accessible to almost any Web browsers.

To export an open movie to another movie format, choose **File**, **Export Movie**. Navigate to the folder to which you will save the file, enter a filename, and then choose a movie format from the **Save as Type** drop-down list.

Aside from generating sequences of static images, or "exporting" to Flash's own format, you have three export options: AVI, QuickTime, and Animated GIF.

AVI and QuickTime provide better quality movies than Animated GIFs. But they also create larger files. Animated GIF files can be viewed in Internet

Nitty Gritty Stuff

What Features Can I Export?

Not all features in a Flash movie export to all movie formats. Actions attached to frames and buttons do not export to AVI format or animated GIF movies, but some actions do export to QuickTime movies.

265

Explorer or Netscape Navigator versions 2 and later. Any Windows user can view AVI files, and any Macintosh user can view QuickTime movies.

Exporting to Windows AVI Format

If you export your movie to Windows' AVI file format, the AVI Export dialog box, shown in Figure 22.7, allows you to choose the size of the movie, the color format, and the sound format. You can also apply compression (to reduce file size) and use the Smooth check box to eliminate jagged edges on diagonal lines.

Figure 22.7

Exporting a video to AVI format makes it available to anyone using a Windows operating system. A 24 bit color movie will be something like three times as large (in file size) as an 8 bit color movie.

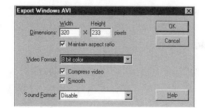

The dimensions that appear by default reflect the size needed to capture your entire movie in the AVI format, so you will probably not want to mess with them. If you do, use the Maintain Aspect Ratio check box to keep the height/width proportions the same as you resize the movie.

The **Video Format** drop-down menu allows you to choose between 8, 16, 24, and 32 bit color. Eight bit color is almost always sufficient to preserve the colors in Flash movies, and saves file space.

The **Sound Format** drop-down menu allows you to choose the sound quality for your video. Flash will suggest a sound format based on the content of the sound files in your movie (and will suggest Disable if you have no sound files in your movie). You can decrease file size by choosing a lower Mhz or bit value, and you can experiment to see if sound quality is still good enough when exported to a smaller file. Or, just accept the recommended sound format for best results.

After you have selected dimensions, video format, and sound format, click **OK** in the Export Window's AVI dialog box. This opens the Video Compression dialog box. The Microsoft Video 1 compression package works with AVI files, and if you select it, you'll see the options in Figure 22.8.

Figure 22.8

Higher video compression creates smaller exported movie files, but reduces movie quality. Compressing this movie 75%—as shown here— reduced the file size from 4,000 KB to 600 KB.

Backstage Pass

Compression Helps

Because AVI is a bitmap, not a vector-based format, exported AVI movies are large. So compression often helps create exported movies with manageable download times. It is often necessary to experiment with AVI videos—especially if they are being published to Web pages—to judge acceptable download times and quality. Add compression to reduce download time. Reduce compression to improve picture quality.

Exporting to QuickTime Movie Format

To export a movie to the QuickTime file format, choose **File**, **Export Movie**. Enter a filename, choose a destination folder, and click **OK**.

The QuickTime Export dialog box, shown in Figure 22.9, allows you to manage quite a few features from your Flash movie. The Dimensions boxes allow you to size the movie, but other features in the dialog box allow you additional control over how your movie is converted to a QuickTime file.

The **Alpha** drop-down menu allows you to control how your Flash movie fits into existing QuickTime tracks. The **Layer** drop-down menu determines what kind of transparency to assign to the Flash background color when the movie is embedded on top of a QuickTime movie.

Figure 22.9

Quicktime videos are relatively faithful to the original Flash movie, and accessible to Macintosh users.

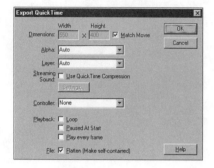

The Use QuickTime Compression check box applies QuickTime compression to audio. The **Controller** drop-down menu allows you to select different QuickTime Controller panels. The Quicktime VR controls are illustrated in Figure 22.10.

Figure 22.10

When you export a movie to Quicktime format, you can elect to embed different types of play controls, including the VCR-style play button in the VR controls option.

The Loop, Paused at Start, and Play Every Frame check boxes control how and when a movie plays when it opens in the QuickTime Viewer. The Flatten check box reduces file size by creating a one-layer movie in QuickTime.

Exporting to Animated GIF

To export a Flash movie to the Animated GIF format, choose **File**, **Export Movie**. Enter a filename and navigate to a destination folder, and choose Animated GIF (*.gif) from the Save as Type drop-down menu. Then click **Save** to open the Export GIF dialog box.

The Export GIF dialog box doesn't have as many control options as Quicktime or AVI provide, but you can choose to loop the movie in the Animations box, as shown in Figure 22.11.

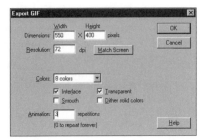

Figure 22.11

Entering a value in the Animations area of the Export to GIF dialog box will show a movie only a defined number of times. After the movies runs the defined number of times, it freezes to display only the final frame.

Use the dimension boxes to change movie size if necessary. The default 72 dpi setting is fine for animated GIF movies. The Colors drop-down menu allows you to choose how many colors to include in the image color palette, and the Interlace, Smooth, Transparent, and Dither Solid Colors check boxes can be used to apply those attributes to the Animated GIF.

Animated GIF Movie Options

Interlacing "fades in" images as they download. *Smoothing* eliminates jagged edges in diagonal lines. *Transparency* makes the movie background color transparent so the movie plays directly against the Web page background. *Dithering* generates colors not included in the movie color palette.

The Animation box allows you to define how many times the movie will repeat (a setting of 0 repeats the movie forever).

Exporting Sound Files

You can extract and export sound files from your movies. Sound files can be saved in the WAV file format.

To export sound files from a video, choose **File**, **Export Movie**. Enter a filename, and navigate to a folder in the **Save In** box. Choose WAV from the **Save as Type** drop-down menu.

After you click **Save**, the Export Windows dialog box appears. Flash will suggest a sound format in the **Sound Format** drop-down menu that best matches your sound file. Use the Ignore Event Sounds check box if you don't want to export sounds attached to events.

After you define your sound file settings, click OK to export the sound file from your movie.

Soundtrack Audio

All the sound files in your movie get merged into a single exported sound file.

The Least You Need to Know

➤ Any frame in a Flash movie can be exported to a graphics image format like GIF or JPEG.

➤ Flash movies can be exported to image sequences—creating a graphics image file for every single frame in the movie.

➤ You can export Flash movies to QuickTime, Windows AVI, or Animated GIF formats.

➤ Sounds can be extracted from movies, and exported as WAV sound files.

Flash-Speak

Flash has its own language. Movies? Vectors? Keyframes? And when you work with Flash, you'll need a smattering of Web-speak as well (GIF, URL, HTML). When you get confused or frustrated, use these quick definitions to keep your head on straight.

Action   An event or activity associated with a movie frame or a button.

ActionScript   Programming code generated by Flash when you assign actions.

Adobe Illustrator   A program for creating vector graphics.

Alignment   Lining objects up in row or column, horizontally or vertically.

Animated GIFS   Movies created by displaying multiple GIF file images in sequence.

Animation   Creating the effect of motion by rapidly displaying many frames of a Flash movie.

Anti-Aliasing   Removing jagged edges from text or graphics.

AVI   Video for Windows files, supported on most Windows machines.

Bit Depth   The number of colors a graphic image is saved with. Eight-bit files hold 256 colors; 24-bit graphics can display over 16 million colors.

Bitmap   An image defined by individual pixels in a format like GIF, JPEG, or TIFF.

BMP   A Windows-compatible bitmap graphics file format.

Browser   The programs that display Web pages, like Netscape Navigator or Internet Explorer.

Browser-Safe Colors   Colors that match the 216 color palette available through browsers.

Button   A graphics object that reacts to being hovered over or clicked in a Flash movie.

Clipboard   Your operating system stores objects copied to memory in the Clipboard, from which they can be pasted.

Conditional Actions   Actions in a browser or Flash movie that depend on a variable.

CorelDRAW   A program for creating vector graphics.

Dither   Create a color by combining pixels from two other colors.

Download   Transferring a file from a server to a browser.

Enhanced Metafile   A graphics file format.

EPS   PostScript—a file format for text and graphics.

Event   An action that triggers a result in an interactive animation. For example, hovering over a button can trigger an action, as can clicking on a button.

Eyedropper   The tool used to grab a color from one object and apply it to another.

Fill   The color or gradient in an object.

Flash Player   A standalone program that allows you to present Flash movies to anyone.

Font   A typeface set for text.

Frame   An individual set of images that displays as part of a Flash movie. Flash movies are created by displaying many frames.

Frame Rate   The speed at which frames are displayed—faster frame rates produce smoother animation.

GIF   A Web-compatible graphics file format that allows transparency and interlacing.

Gradient   A fill that merges two or more colors gradually, producing a rainbow-like fill.

Grid   Lines that display on the Flash stage for aligning objects, but are not displayed in movies.

Group   Temporarily combined objects are grouped to move or edit them all at once.

Hot Spot   An area on a button that triggers an action when hovered over or clicked.

HTML   HyperText Markup Language—the basic code that allows browsers to interpret Web pages.

Interactive   Objects that react to a user, for example by displaying information, or opening a new Web page.

Instance   An appearance of a symbol in a movie. Symbols can have multiple instances in movies.

Interlacing   A process for allowing GIF images to display in low resolution as they are downloaded into a browser.

Internet   The global infrastructure that connects browsers to Web sites.

Java   A programming language recognized by many Web browsers.

JavaScript   A programming language used to create interactivity and animation.

JPEG   A Web-compatible graphics file format often used to display photos.

Kerning   Changing spacing between text characters.

Keyframe   A frame that denotes a change in an animated sequence.

Lasso   The Lasso tool in Flash is used to select an irregular area and all the objects in that area.

Layer   Flash movies are usually composed of many overlayed layers, each of which is transparent but can be edited separately.

Link   Text or an object in a Web page that opens another Web page or Web file.

Mask   A masked layer is a layer with holes in it, like the eyes, nose, and mouth of a mask. These holes allow you to reveal part but not all of underlying layers.

MIME   A file type for compressing large files.

Morphing   Transforming a shape through animation.

Motion Path   A line along which objects move in an animation.

Movie   In Flash, files with all their component parts are referred to as movies.

Movie-Clip   An animation saved as a symbol so it can be reused in a movie.

MP3   A sound file format.

Object   A single graphics element in Flash.

Paint Bucket   The tool that assigns colors to objects.

Palette   A set of colors.

Panel   Flash 5 features a set of 17 panels, each of which allows you to control different elements of a movie.

PICT   A Macintosh-compatible graphics file format.

Pixel   The dots that make up a monitor screen—normally 72 to an inch.

PNG   A Web-compatible graphics file format similar to GIF, but not was widely recognized by browsers.

Publish   Create an HTML page to present a Flash movie.

QuickTime   A movie format supported by most Macintosh machines.

Rotate   Spinning an object by rotating one of its corners clockwise or counter-clockwise.

Scale   To scale an object is to resize it.

Scene   A component of a Flash movie—a set of saved frames.

Select   The Select tool allows you to choose one or more objects to move or modify.

Skew   Distort an object by moving parallel lines in opposite directions.

Snap   Enables objects to stick to set points on the Stage.

Sound   An audio file that plays as part of a Flash animation.

Stage   The drawing area that fills the bulk of the Flash window.

Streaming   A technique that allows Flash movies to begin to play in a browser even as they are being downloaded from a server.

SWF   The file format for Flash movies.

Symbol   An image, animation, or button that can be reused in a movie. Each time a symbol is used it is referred to as an instance.

Tag   An HTML code command.

Text   Lettering objects created with the Text tool, which can be converted to shapes.

Text Field   A text box that collects and saves data.

Timeline   The area on top of the Stage in Flash that controls which frame you work in.

Transparency   Transparent color fills allow some of the object that they cover to display.

Tweening   Automating the process of animation by letting Flash create sequential frames that blend from one frame to another.

URL   Uniform Resource Locator—the address of a Web site.

Vector   Vector-based graphics rely on calculated lines and curves rather than individual bitmapped pixels to define lines and shapes.

WAV   A sound file format.

Web   The World Wide Web—the global network of Web sites.

Wireframe   A memory efficient way to display just the outline of objects in Flash.

XML   A simplified version of HTML.

Index